Enjoy the Read!
Mimi Barash
Coppersmith

EAT FIRST, CRY LATER

The Life Lessons of a First-Generation College
Graduate, Penn State Alumna and Female CEO

by **MIMI BARASH COPPERSMITH**

CONTENTS

PREFACE

This book has been a dream in the making since my first husband died in 1975. As you can imagine, I've had many people's advice and support along the way. I started writing in earnest in 1989, after my second husband's death. At that time, it was part of my overall healing, and once I'd gotten enough of my story out to move forward, I did just that. I returned to the idea of sharing my life story in 2001 and worked with three different editors over the next fifteen years, struggling to finish.

Then, the Sunday after Thanksgiving 2016, I was sitting with my older daughter, Carol, at her kitchen table, and we got talking about this project, which she has always believed in.

"I'd really like to finish it next year," I said, "You've helped so many other people tell their stories. Could you help me finish mine?"

Carol said, "Mom, I'd love to help you tell your story."

We made a promise to finish the book and get my story out into the world by my eighty-fifth birthday in 2018.

For a long time, I really didn't think people would be interested in my story; I thought of myself as an investigative journalist at the intersection of others' lives, rather than the narrator of my own story. But, I must confess, I am tickled that I am finally telling my story to other people, especially to other women. This story is recounted from my own perspective, as a woman, daughter, sister, mother, grandmother, friend, community member, and leader.

Everything I did, whether I wanted to or not, I did as a woman. I came of age at a time when barriers were breaking down. Gender, race, sexuality: all of these changed profoundly in my local community while I was running a business with my husband, raising our daughters, and then pulling my life back together as a single mother after my husband died. I became a feminist as the movement gained momentum in the 1970s, and my own daughters and granddaughters inspire me to continue breaking barriers and making a difference for other women.

It is in that spirit that I bring this book into the world in my eighty-fifth year of life. I came to Penn State in 1950, the first in my family to graduate from college. I have lived my entire adult life in the same town where I was a first-generation college student, at the intersection of Penn State and State College—what I call "town and gown."

Penn State and State College made me lucky. I received a great education, had access to world-class health care, and lived in a community where I was valued and able to thrive as who I am.

To thank Penn State and keep it going for the next generation, all profits from the sale of this book will go to support Study Abroad in the Donald P. Bellisario College of Communications at Pennsylvania State University. I believe that opportunities to study abroad are to this generation what attending college was for mine: a way to open yourself to a wider world, to meet people with different experiences, to learn and build new opportunities together.

I hope you enjoy the journey that was—and is—life with Mimi.

CHAPTER 1
DON'T LET LIFE STEP ON YOU: GROWING UP IN KINGSTON, PENNSYLVANIA

I am ten years old. I run home from the Jewish Community Center in Wilkes-Barre, where I was playing basketball after school with some boys. The dining room table is full: full of food, full of cousins, full of noise. I wash my hands at the kitchen sink; I slow down, catch my breath, and take my mother's chair, as she gets up to start washing dishes.

"Mimi, why are you always late?" my mother yells from the kitchen, not really angry but loud. I don't answer her. She's moving quickly. I start eating what's left—roast chicken, with the potatoes and carrots cooked in the same pan—chewing very slowly so I won't have to help with the dishes. The aunts and uncles are talking quickly, interrupting one another. I listen to them without looking up from my plate, and under the table my hands trace the designs of a tablecloth my mother embroidered herself.

"We haven't heard from him in two weeks…"

"They are killing Jews in those camps…"

"Roosevelt is not doing enough…"

***

As far back as my memory reaches, my family proudly embraced the rich traditions and harrowing history of our religion, with all its controversies and horrific, unwarranted hardships. My siblings and I were never spared the unpleasant realities that shaped our family's background and the life consequences we faced because we were Jews. We were outsiders in Kingston, a bit at odds with the main community, in ways I carry with me even today.

1

***

My journey began on June 11, 1933 at the Wilkes-Barre General Hospital in northeastern Pennsylvania. My parents brought me home to our cramped house in Kingston, across the Susquehanna River from Wilkes-Barre. The Great Depression held the country in its grip, and Hitler had been appointed Chancellor of Germany.

I was the fourth child, and third girl, born to Max (1895 - 1956) and Tillie Landau Ungar (1901 - 1990), Jewish immigrants who fled the spreading anti-Semitism of Eastern Europe in the early twentieth century. My parents had been introduced to one another by my mother's brother, Nat Landau, in the way many Jewish families matched one another with people they already knew. It was a time when few doors were open for Jewish immigrants to integrate into the larger community. Max and Tillie met frequently at the YMHA and eloped to New York in 1920 because my mother's father did not want them to get married.

My parents ran a small grocery store, Capitol Grocery, in Wilkes-Barre, where we all worked after school and on weekends: everything from unpacking boxes of produce to helping at the cash register. With minimal formal education before they came to the U.S. in their teens, my parents expected us to study hard and excel in all we did. We were told to stand up for ourselves and for our heritage. Though we were of quite humble means compared to our neighbors and cousins, because we owned a grocery store we always had food. And my mom was a great cook who loved having people over, so our dining room was always full of people and food. We were taught to appreciate all that we had, to be scrappy and always learning—from the good as well as the bad in life. Max and Tillie taught us to be proud of who we were, to respect others and to help those less fortunate than ourselves. My father often said, "Mimi, you can change the world if you put your whole mind into your work." It is no surprise that I developed a motivated and competitive spirit early in life.

My parents named me Marian, but when I was very ill as a baby, my first cousin, Rose Engel, who was old enough to be my grandmother and nursed me back to health, called me "Mimi." And I've been Mimi—pronounced "Mimmy" not "MeeMee"—ever since.

My three older siblings, Sylvia (1921 - 1974), Calvin (1925 - 1944), and Yetta (1929 - 2015), and I, each in our own ways, worked to live up to our parents' confidence in us, as well as their relentless drive to succeed in their new country. Thanks to our particular upbringing, my siblings and I recognized the responsibility and respect we owed to our family, friends, faith, and community. Learning the importance of relationships early on influenced my life's trajectory in myriad positive ways.

Seven months after my birth, my parents assumed custodial responsibility for two of my first cousins, sixteen-year-old Ruth and her twelve-year-old brother Fred Grossman. They came to us from New York City when tragedy struck their family. Their mother, my father's older sister, had died of influenza, and their father was deemed incapable of performing the demanding task of single-parenthood.

Ruth and Fred lived with us—six children in our tiny, three-bedroom, one-bathroom house. There was absolutely no private or personal space, and we all shared one tiny closet in the hall. Often, until I was eight, I could not sleep through the night without wetting my bed. I shared a bed with my sister Yetta, who would say, "It's ok Mimi, I'll help you clean it up." My mother would yell at me and hang the wet, yellow sheets out in the backyard where our neighbors could see them.

Due to the sheer volume of people, we bathed on a pre-set schedule once a week. Our house was tight and crowded, the intensity and proximity of other people too much for all of us sometimes. I'm told that Sylvia, my eldest sister, who was twelve at the time Ruth and Fred moved in, did not adjust to our cousins' adoption into our family. Growing up, it seemed to me as though Sylvia picked fights with everyone, enjoyed the sparring and drama, and never understood—as I felt I did—that we were doing what had to be done by adding these two new people to our already packed home.

My older brother Calvin, the only son, grew up to be the All-American Jewish boy—the one who could do no wrong. Calvin carried this reputation in every facet of life. Cal was the person we turned to in times of need. He was simultaneously a brother, a trusted friend, and a mediator of the many disputes in our packed and noisy home. He was the valedictorian of his graduating class at Kingston High School. From Boy Scouts to the U.S. Army Air Corps to becoming a navigator on a B-17 in World War II, Calvin was a dutiful son and someone who took the time to help those around him. He would come home, sit down next to me on the couch, and ask me about my friends and schoolwork. Eight years my senior, Calvin made me feel safe and protected.

In 1943, at age eighteen, Calvin convinced our mother that he must enlist in the war effort. Though as an only son he did not technically need to serve, he believed this was a necessary decision to protect our country and avenge the innocent victims at Pearl Harbor.

My mother eventually relented, whispering, "God should cut off my hand for having signed this paper."

Calvin sent us what they called "V-mail" several times a week. It was lightweight red, white and blue paper in a self-sealed envelope that came with the regular mail. When a letter came, we all scrambled to get to it first. His voice and inspiring presence came through so clearly in each letter, filled with exciting stories and upbeat news from the war effort. "How is the little politician?" he asked me in one, "I'm sure you're leading your class as you always do!"

And then the mail stopped. No one received mail from "Sonny" in nearly two weeks. I'd run to the mailbox, and then sulk into the house when I found it empty. If I asked the adults why there was no mail from Calvin, they pushed me away gruffly.

It's July 25, 1945, and I was spending a few days at my Aunt Jenny Landau's summer home on Harveys Lake in the Poconos. I was still asleep when my aunt tiptoed into the bedroom that my cousin Sally, my sister Yetta, and I shared.

She whispered, "Come on, girls. Wake up. We've got to go home."

When I asked why, she acted like she didn't hear me. That eleven-mile car ride seemed an eternity.

Pulling up to our home at 119 Third Avenue, I sensed something different in the air. I saw my Aunt Clara's two-door, black Plymouth parked out front. In my mind, my aunt's black car always suggested bad news. My mother rushed onto our front porch, crying and waving her arms, as if she were a bird who would prefer to be flying away. She screamed the heart-wrenching news to the world:

"Calvin is gone! Our Calvin is gone."

The telegram from the U.S. War Department explained, "The Secretary of War desires to express his deep regret that your son Second Lieutenant Calvin S Ungar was killed in action on seven July over Italy."

July 25, 1944 remains indelibly etched in my memory, a day when my life changed forever. After this, our home—always so alive and full of activity, even during the fiercest arguments—suddenly collapsed into a grotto of sorrow. Scores of people filtered in and out, offering boundless food and comfort in their attempts to fill the gaping hole in our hearts.

***

I read the telegram with my own eyes, I took it in, and out of the chaos and pain, I chose to help others. I can still remember sitting at the top of the wooden stairs, listening to the relentless cycle of sobbing and consoling. Alone at the top of those steps, I developed a sudden, uncontrollable urge to help my parents overcome their devastating grief. I felt that was what Calvin would want me to do. I would make myself happy by making them happy; I would make them happy by doing my best in everything, just as my brother had done. It's not that I had those thoughts exactly. But I became the person I am today when we began the terrible thing that was continuing life without someone we had counted on to hold so many things together.

Tragedy has a way of shaping who we are as individuals. My brother's death, then and now, is the single incident that has had the most profound impact on my direction in life. At a young age, I learned that life is filled with losses that feel unendurable. But somehow you go on.

At eleven years old, I had no measurable experience, no credentials and no direction. But I had the drive to make life better, and that was enough to bring happiness back into a home cursed with the death of an amazing, young son. These changes required me to try new things and grow in new ways; my relationships to others changed, my relationship to myself changed. I took on sports and debate, as Calvin had done, and became the one my father took to boxing matches and basketball games after work.

I continue to share the story of my brother's death with others—particularly women—who desire to embark on a transformative journey towards self-contentment, confidence, and success. I learned that I could overcome the crushing weight of adversity by expanding and flourishing for myself and then giving of myself to other people.

My matter-of-fact mother's advice was simple:

Lesson #1: "Don't let anyone step on you. Don't let life step on you."

She might have said, "Eat first, cry later." It's certainly an idea she inspired.

From my mother, I learned both the courage and spirit to keep moving forward, and the reminder to take care of yourself and others first, and then, over time, to let the sadness and horror work its way through.

***

Unexpected assistance entered my life eleven months later when my baby brother, Sanford Jerome Ungar, was born on June 10, 1945, the day before my twelfth birthday. To me, his arrival was magically joyful, diverting my family from the sadness that surrounded everything after Calvin's death. "Sandy" was like a gift to me, a person I cherished from the moment he arrived, and someone about whom it is hard for me to feel anything but boundless gratitude and pride to this day. By the time my two older sisters moved away in the late 1940s, my father was quite ill from diabetes, and my friendship with Sandy was deepened through a shared sense of responsibility for our aging parents.

Sandy still reminds me of my first day of college, the day I "deserted" him in front of the New College Diner on College Avenue. He was five years old when my parents drove the three hours from Kingston to State College and dropped me off at Penn State.

He screamed, yelled, and made a huge fuss, crying out, "Mimi, don't leave me!" as our forlorn parents drove back home. For me, Penn State was the great liberation my soul required; I dove into my education and my new community with every aspect of my being and never looked back.

PENN STATE'S
GRAND NATIONAL FORENSIC CHAMPIONS
1953

MIMI UNGAR   LOIS LEHMAN   JANE MONTGOMERY   GUYLA WOODWARD
...ONES PORTER   SUSAN HOLTZINGER   SALLY LOWRY   MARY JANE KELLEY
COACH   CLAYTON H SCHUG

1. My parents, Tillie and Max Ungar.

2. My brother, Calvin Ungar, at his high school graduation.

3. The telegram we received July 25, 1944.

4. My proudest moment at Penn State when our team won the Women's Grand National Debating Championship in 1953.

5. With my debate teammate, Dr. Lois Pulver Krop ('52), from Wilkes-Barre.

6. My wedding to Sy Barash in 1954.

THE 1950s

In 1950, Penn State was a college. In 1953, the year I graduated, it became a university. Every aspect of the town and campus were transforming in the 1950s, and I was, too. I'd never stepped foot on the Penn State campus before I arrived to begin my freshman year on an unseasonably cold, rainy day in August, 1950. Once, on a high school debate trip to Franklin, Pennsylvania, we stopped at the Corner Room for lunch, and I saw the main campus gate across the street. I was so impressed with the Corner Room: the wooden booths and the bustle of people in and out. That was all I knew about college before I landed there that day.

***

My dorm, McAllister Hall, was the first women's dorm when Penn State began admitting women during the war. There were annoying rules limiting women's freedom in the 1950s: a silly dress code forbidding shorts or jeans on campus; permission required to go out of town (even to Bellefonte, the county seat); and a 10 p.m. curfew. The housemothers enforced these rules strictly. When someone was a few minutes late and the front door was locked, she'd knock on a first-floor window, hoping someone would let her in to avoid being caught.

***

The first semester, I concentrated on my studies. I had quiet misgivings about my ability to make the grade in college, even though I was among the top performers at Kingston High School. I felt a deep sense of being less prepared than the students whose parents could afford tutors and prep classes. Most of my Jewish friends were privileged to

9

attend Wyoming Seminary, a highly respected Methodist prep school in Kingston. Even in those days, there was a palpable difference between the students whose parents had money and those of us without it—in the schools we could attend and the opportunities our parents could afford to give us outside of school.

Upon doing well in my general education courses (Art Appreciation, English, Math, and French) that first semester, I jumped into the deep end of the pool with numerous activities. I decided to major in Journalism and started reporting on the president's office for *The Daily Collegian*. I also joined the women's intramural basketball team (women played half court in those days) and sold food to other students in my dorm through a concession called Sally's Snacks. The company owned a restaurant in town. They delivered a big metal basket, about three feet long, and I set up the concession outside the house mother's apartment, selling tuna fish, egg salad, turkey, and ham and cheese sandwiches, as well as snacks and drinks three nights a week. I made a twenty percent commission, about ten dollars a night.

Running that Sally's Snacks concession late at night, I met over one hundred girls. They were from places I'd never heard of all over Pennsylvania, towns with names like Latrobe, Conshohocken, and Port Matilda. Some of them had grown up on farms; others were from affluent Pittsburgh and Philadelphia suburbs, and many were, like me, children of immigrants. The war was in the past, and the campus was loaded with veterans. We shared an excitement about what was ahead.

All my days (and long nights) at *The Daily Collegian* taught me about thoroughness and accuracy and made me a more responsible person. My *Collegian* run peaked spring semester 1953, when I served as editorial director and got paid for my weekly column, "Strictly from Ungar."

I decided to join Phi Sigma Sigma sorority, one of three Jewish sororities, and the one that attracted the less affluent students. I wasn't what you'd call a typical sorority woman: I was much more active around campus than I was in the sorority. I used Phi Sigma Sigma as a place to make friends and talk after all my other work was done. Whether over a late-night tuna sandwich or bridge game, it was where I learned how to be a member of the larger community by interacting and just hanging out and talking things through with other women.

***

Just before the end of my spring semester in 1953, I met Sy Barash, who took me on a first date to Friday night services at Hillel. Seven years my senior, he had stories from the war, which reminded me of my brother Calvin, and he was already on his way in business, having just joined Sid Friedman ('42) in a new advertising company, Friedman and Barash, earlier that year.

We were married less than a year later, on January 31, 1954. When I married, I thought of myself first and foremost as a journalist. I had started a Master's program in Speech at Penn State and loved both the teaching and the small, graduate classes. But life had other plans for me. Sy and I moved into our first house in 1956, brought our first daughter, Carol, home in 1958, and started our own advertising business in the basement of that house in 1959. It was the house my children grew up in and the house they left when they went away to college.

***

In 1956, I lost my father, who had been struggling with progressive, debilitating diabetes for more than a decade. Before he became ill, when I was just eight or nine years old, he had taken me to baseball games, basketball games and boxing matches, making me a great sports fan. I worked very closely with him in the store. He knew that I didn't like the dirty jobs--like bagging potatoes--so he let me work the cash register. It was my goal to come out to the exact penny. I hear him saying, "Great job, Mimi. You stuck with it until it was right. Great job." Soon after Calvin became a soldier, my father had passed out in our grocery store and was never really himself again. He was a veteran of World War I and received his treatments at the Veterans Hospital in Wilkes-Barre.

***

When Milton Eisenhower arrived as the eleventh president of the Pennsylvania State College in the fall of 1950, I was a freshman, living in McAllister Hall. With the help of his brother Dwight, who became U.S. president in 1953, Milton Eisenhower would expand every aspect of Penn State, even the highways in and out of town.

11

In 1953, when the Pennsylvania State College became the Pennsylvania State University, the local community defeated a referendum to change the name of the town. Eisenhower applied for a separate postal code for the university and had faculty, staff, and alumni select the new name. The choices included Atherton, Centre Hills, Mount Nittany, and University Park, the last of which was selected.

Eric Walker, Penn State's strong and steady twelfth president from 1956 to 1971, arrived during World War II as a prominent engineer in the war effort, bringing his entire underwater research lab with him from Harvard. Eisenhower and Walker transformed Penn State into a nationally prominent research university that also nurtured excellence in athletics and the arts.

Just across College Avenue, State College grew dramatically in the 1950s, ever so slowly becoming more diverse. On January 1, 1948, Penn State football players Wally Triplett ('49) and Dennie Hoggard ('49) were the first African-Americans to play in the Cotton Bowl, but they couldn't get a haircut in State College. My husband Sy was among those who worked to change that, by promising to use the one local barber who would agree to let black men in the door. But State College was still quite monolithic: politically very conservative, almost completely white and Christian.

The physical boundaries of State College were expanding. J. Alvin Hawbaker led the development of Park Forest Village, an innovative planned community in "the barrens" on the north side of town. Hawbaker was one of many successful business people, leaders in the local community, who had tremendous entrepreneurial spirit and drive but little formal education. Then there were many, like myself and my husband Sy, who were the first in our families to get a college education and for whom Penn State changed every aspect of our being. Unlike the area where I grew up, where I felt very self-consciously Jewish, at Penn State I could apply to any job and participate in every activity. It didn't matter that I was Jewish.

There were a few people, like our neighbor Jim Palmer, who had graduate training in engineering and the sciences and saw—long before others—the tremendous technological breakthroughs that lay ahead as we integrated computing and data-driven science and communication into our everyday lives. We shared a very positive sense that many things were changing, and all for the better.

12

CHAPTER 2
GET INVOLVED: MY EARLY LESSONS FROM DEBATE AND JOURNALISM

When I embarked for State College to begin my freshman year early Sunday morning, August 27, 1950, all my belongings were stuffed into two suitcases in the trunk of our gray four-door, stick-shift Plymouth. Close behind us, my roommate, Sylvia May Davis ('54), followed with her parents. Sylvia and I were friends from Kingston High School and the Jewish Community Center. The raw, rainy day did nothing to lessen my excitement over beginning the next phase of life.

***

As we drove to State College, I thought to myself, again and again, "You will be the *first* in the family... *if* you graduate..."

***

My father was wearing a gray Stetson hat. He was pretty sick by this point, but still driving. A few inches shorter than my mother and chunky, he rarely raised his voice. He had a long gray overcoat, the same one he'd worn for over twenty years. I was wearing a blue and white polka dot skirt and shirt, a matching set I bought at a discount at my cousin Sam Rothman's store in Pittston. This was the first of many blue and white outfits I'd purchase over the years. But that outfit was rayon and shrank from the downpour during our move-in to McAllister Hall, never to be worn again.

Our third-floor dorm started as a challenge on move-in day—up and down, up and down the steps. My father couldn't walk up the stairs, but my mother tried. I didn't want her to help me too much.

She wore all black clothes and spoke in a very loud voice. She wanted to take care of things I wanted to do for myself—like unpacking and hanging my clothes in my very own walk-in closet.

Spacious, clean, and comfortable, my room was much bigger than any place I'd ever lived before, nicer than I expected, and conveniently located on the middle of campus next to Old Main, which housed classrooms and administrative offices. Communal bathrooms and pay phones dotted the hallways. I could shower any time, and no one listened in when I called my new friends. Besides clothes, the only things in my suitcases were my dictionary and thesaurus. I had a laundry box that I mailed home every two weeks; my mother mailed it back with everything neatly pressed and folded. By the time I was a senior they had installed laundromats in the basement.

***

As soon as I felt confident that I could handle the academic work at Penn State, I began branching out and getting involved in the college and larger State College community. I learned such important life lessons from the world-class extra-curricular activities at Penn State, especially journalism and debate.

Lesson #2: Take advantage of the activities that are right in front of you—whatever your age—to learn, to meet people who challenge you, and to make a demonstrable difference in the lives of others in your community.

I began participating in debate in high school. My high school debate coach, Mr. Bennett, taught us to respond quickly and concisely. This made me a fighter verbally, a skill that helped me plan and win contests that seemed almost insurmountable, much later, when I was running my own business. It was a special bonus during my high school debates when my father skipped work and slipped quietly into a seat in the back of the auditorium.

At Penn State, we debated issues that are still hot button issues today: the abolition of the Electoral College and capital punishment are both topics I researched and debated nearly seventy years ago! We had to be prepared to argue both sides of these contentious issues and to back up our arguments with specific facts.

After competing fiercely in tryouts for the Penn State women's debate team my sophomore year, Professor Clayton Schug called us all back in and told us who had made the cut. A physically small man, Mr. Schug had a way of bringing out the best in each of us. He named me the team manager my third year, in 1953, and that same year, we won the women's Grand National Debate Championships. That is one of my most cherished honors, because we competed with schools of much higher academic stature than Penn State, but I had this deep sense that we would beat them all.

Mr. Schug found excuses for me to do odd jobs for him, so he could pay me. He and his wife, Josie, and their daughter Marcia ('62) invited me over for dinner and treated me like one of their own children. I always felt that he was looking out for me, that he knew my family had very little money and that I was working my way through Penn State with very little to spare.

I would dash from debate practice in the Sparks Building to the *Collegian* newsroom in the Carnegie Building. The newsroom rivaled a small city newspaper in noise and intensity. The ticker tape competed with the sounds of multiple typewriters pounding as Penn State students produced an award-winning newspaper every day. In those days, all the student bosses at the *Collegian* were men with strong voices and opinions: Marvin Krasnansky ('52), Ron Bonn ('52), Ray Galant ('52) and David Jones ('53).

Tough as those guys were, I credit them for encouraging me to compete and excel. Over time, I became a member of the *Collegian* senior board and ultimately Editorial Director. I wrote a weekly column, "Strictly from Ungar," where I enjoyed stirring the pot on race relations, the student side of contentious issues with the college, and generally looking out for the underdog.

Looking back, I see how interested I was in people who were struggling, as I was. I led a campaign to raise money for Larry Sharp, a student who was paralyzed in a trampoline accident. I became friends with Joe, a Native American who was the janitor in my dorm and who helped me navigate the campus.

My Jewish heritage was important in forming my character; Penn State opened me to a much wider world of relationships than my close knit, homogenous childhood. Before Penn State, I had never lived under the same roof or eaten daily meals with people who were not Jewish. Suddenly, we all got our food from one line, and we all spent time together, just eating.

There was so much to do at Penn State! It was all such an extraordinary gift for someone like me, a poor girl from a small town, whose parents believed in education but had very little of their own. I felt I had really arrived when I was listed in the 1951-52 *Who's Who in the News at Penn State College*, a classified student booklet printed by Commercial Printing, which was owned at the time by my future husband's business partner, Sid Friedman. At Penn State, I began my lifelong juggling act, what Sy called "Mimi's running," cramming as much as I possibly could into every minute of every single day.

CHAPTER 3
SAVE AND GIVE BACK: THE PUSHKE AND THE COMMUNITY CHEST

Growing up, we lived modestly. Because my parents owned a grocery store, we were never hungry. In fact, around my mother's dinner table, I learned a sense of abundance and the importance of sharing with others.

I also learned to shop frugally, to choose nice things with great care and attention to sales and savings. My mother and I shopped mostly at the Boston Store (now Boscov), our local department store, and the small local shops with Jewish owners. My parents knew all of them, and for a couple of years in high school, I worked part-time at the Lerner Shop, where I got a small discount on my clothes.

My mother usually bought on the layaway plan, making weekly or monthly payments. I often say, "I love monthly payments, can't live without them. All my life, I've had monthly payments." It all started as a girl from modest means shopping with my mother after the war.

In those days, we put our savings into government bonds: you bought a $25 savings bond for $17.50 and put it away to mature. Lots of everyday people did this; it was considered patriotic to save. I now have in my safe deposit box over $15,000 in government savings bonds, because it's a habit and the right thing to do!

There were two rules in our house: you had to save part of what you earned, and you had to give part of it to *tzedakah*—a Jewish word that is usually translated as "charity," but goes much deeper to a sense of gratitude and healing.

To foster giving back, we had a small *pushke* in the kitchen. There's no exact English translation for the Yiddish word *pushke*. Our turquoise and white tin *pushke* hung on the wall, where everyone could reach it. Every month or so a short, chubby man with *paias* (long, curly sideburns based on the Jewish injunction not to cut your hair), an unkempt beard, and a black top hat picked up the money. He had the key to unlock the *pushke*; the funds went mysteriously out of town to help a variety of Jewish causes.

How much we gave was up to us, but whether it was shoveling snow, raking leaves, or babysitting, we had to give part of everything we earned to people who "weren't as lucky as we were." So when I babysat for twenty-five cents an hour, I'd put five cents in there. If I shoveled snow and made a couple of dollars, I'd put in a little more.

The idea of giving back, no matter how modest your means, drew me across College Avenue into State College in the fall of 1952, and I started picking up what I call my "free credits"—all the learning I got as a student from working in the local State College community. My first real job in community organizing was as the publicity manager for the Community Chest, which later became the United Fund and then the United Way. This was my very first project that combined sales, service, and alliance-building.

My role was to get students involved in the Community Chest and to inspire them to give donations every year. I came up with the silly phrase, "All your begs in one ask-it," and set out to raise more money than anyone ever had before. This role took everything I knew from growing up in Kingston, pushing me in an entirely new direction and helping me build relationships in the State College community.

This project was a big leap for me at the time. I was a very different person in high school. I played basketball and softball, and I helped organize a class trip to Washington, DC, the first time that was ever done in Kingston. But, for the most part, I worked on my own, not with lots of other people.

I think many college students, and especially first-generation students, have a similar experience. From the moment I arrived at Penn State, the quality and quantity of people around me changed completely. For me, the local community had as much to do with my overall sense of expansion and learning as the college did. The campus and the community were pretty small and compact, so when I had ideas it was easy to try them out.

As publicity chair for the Community Chest, I started meeting and working with local business people for the first time. From my tight-knit, small-town Jewish childhood, I was trained at an early age to "stick with your own and help your own." So, of course, I went to the one Jewish printer in town and asked for his help and advice.

On a gray fall day in 1952, I walked to Sid Friedman's Commercial Printing shop in the basement of the Glennland Building on Pugh Street and ordered little white scratch pads with Penn State blue lettering: "Put all your begs in one ask-it."

Sid laughed and said, "Where did you get that idea, Mimi?"

"I just thought of it," I said, talking fast, "there are so many different causes. It seems like a great way for students to help all of them."

"I hadn't really thought about it that way, Mimi," he said, "I like the way you think."

CHAPTER 4
PERSONAL LIFE REQUIRES WORK: MARRIED AND
STRUGGLING TO HAVE CHILDREN

I spent the summer of 1952 living on South Harper Street in Chicago with my sister, Sylvia, and her husband Henry. I worked in the publication division at Kling Studios on the North Side, proofreading GE user instruction manuals, my first real job and the only full-time job I ever had reporting to someone who was not myself or my family.

The big lesson of that summer in Chicago was how much work and struggle are woven into the fabric of everyday life. Sylvia worked as a psychiatric nurse in what today is considered gerontology. Henry was a research endocrinologist at Michael Reese Hospital. Sylvia's closest friend was a much older woman whom she had nursed through a long illness.

While I lived with her, Sylvia was coping with a very sick husband. She would come home from work and pour herself Ballantine whiskey "on the rocks." She'd refill the glass a few times, her moods shifting quickly especially when she drank. One day she'd be screaming about our mother; the next day she'd break down in tears, sad and afraid she was going to lose Henry. That summer I was so worried about my sister, and many nights I drank with her.

When Sylvia was happy she was exuberant and very creative. Sylvia played the piano with passion. She took me to art museums for the first time. She had also begun expressing herself in painting—bold, abstract, mixed media works.

***

Henry died two days before my college graduation in August 1953 from complications of polycystic kidneys. Sylvia insisted that I attend my graduation. When I went to visit her the next day, my childhood bedwetting returned; I would dream that a large California redwood was falling on me, and when I woke up my sheets were soaked. I felt humiliated, but Sylvia understood what I could not give voice: that the loss of Henry, another older brother of sorts, made me feel childlike, powerless, and deeply afraid.

***

The day before I met Sy Barash, May 8, 1953, I was feeling low. A junior and running out of money, I thought that I had fallen short of one of my big goals: to be tapped for Mortar Board, the senior women's honorary society recognizing leadership, service, and scholarship. I had been moping around all day, feeling sorry for myself while my sorority sisters tried to cheer me up. I went to bed early and woke to singing outside my dorm window. I assumed they were singing for my roommate, Peggy Crooks ('54), who had already been tapped for Mortar Board. But by the time they finished singing, I realized that I was being tapped as well.

The celebration went on late into the night, including a secret initiation ceremony that included Helen Eisenhower, the wife of the university president, and Pearl O. Weston, the Dean of Women. By the time I got to bed, the sun was up, and I was completely exhausted.

When my Simmons Hall dorm phone rang at 5:10 pm the next day, I was sleeping in the bed closer to the window. By that time every room had its own phone. I answered with a gruff, "Yes?"

The soft, mellow voice on the other end replied gently, "Sorry if I woke you up. This is Sy Barash. I'm calling because the Friedmans and Alexanders thought I'd like to meet you."

Sid's wife, Helen Friedman ('43), and Mimi Alexander, who were advisors to my sorority, had encouraged Sy to call me and ask me out.

"Oh, sorry I answered so rudely," I said as I started to come to. "I was tapped for Mortar Board last night, and I barely slept."

Sy told me his story: He started Penn State at the Lock Haven campus and spent a few months there before enlisting in the Marines in 1943. After the war with the help of the GI Bill, Sy came back to the main campus. He'd graduated from Penn State in the summer of

1950 and had returned to State College to become a partner with Sid and his brother Herman in their small, Central Pennsylvania billboard company, Nittany Ad-Ver-Tis-Er, and an even smaller advertising agency, Friedman and Barash. At age twenty-six, Sy had used his wartime poker winnings and a $5,000 loan from his father to purchase a fifty percent share of Friedman's companies.

"I wondered if you'd like to attend Friday night services with me and my friend, Elliot Krane?"

I remember, thinking, 'What kind of guy asks you out to religious services on your first date?' I told him that I'd been excused from required attendance at services by my sorority, which was the sponsor that evening, because of the Mortar Board celebration the night before.

"They won't mind if you come anyway. Why not join me just so we can meet?" Sy persisted. I liked the sound of his voice, pleasant and self-assured.

"Why not?" I thought. My first real beau had left me when he graduated in 1952, and I hadn't had a serious date in months.

Sy showed up wearing a deep blue, almost black pinstripe suit and tie. His shoes were freshly polished. From the beginning, Sy was very different from the guys I usually dated. At age twenty-six and a veteran, he was already balding, and he was—at most—5'6" tall. He was a tad overweight, with a warm, unforgettable, ear-to-ear grin. He was a bit shy, and spoke in a way that was so kind it felt almost formal.

The first time we met, he shook my hand and said, "I'm so happy to meet you, Mimi, you come highly recommended."

"Pleased to meet you too, Sy," I played along, letting him take the lead.

Our first date was not auspicious. But Sy persisted. He wore me down by letting me talk about myself. Eventually, he got a second date, and then a third, and we went out frequently that summer.

Sy was a great thinker and learner, not a great student. But his personality was larger than life; few people who met Sy forgot him.

I enjoyed dating a townie and businessman. He would be off on business calls or scouting billboard locations all day, while I headed to class and my extracurricular responsibilities. Then, after work and classes, we would meet and go out—to a movie or for a drive. We spent weekends together at Whipple Dam, a popular swimming and boating destination across the mountain in Huntington County.

Looking back, I remember doing most of the talking, while Sy listened seriously to my nineteen-year-old chatter. This kind attention from a man who had picked his way through the ruins of a bombed city on the other side of the world made me feel I was truly special. Honestly, in Sy's eyes, I believe I was the best version of myself. Even on my worst days, even when we fought, I could sense his love for me and his belief in my ability to make a difference, not just for him but for the world.

I do not take this for granted: many women lack this sense of wholeness with their life partners, or they lose it over time. Sy was, from our first date to his last day, my biggest champion, my advocate, ally, and friend.

That spring and summer, I packed my schedule with the classes I needed to graduate early. I sent out applications to the leading graduate schools in Journalism. Though I was accepted to all of them, I couldn't begin to afford the tuition and travel. At the time, there were almost no scholarships for graduate education. So I decided to stay at Penn State, where I received a small teaching assistantship and a tiny scholarship, to pursue a double Masters in Speech and Journalism.

I graduated in August, a year early, and moved to an apartment above Metzger's, the old bookstore on Allen Street (where Rapid Transit is today), with Rosalie Eisenstein from Kingston, who was an undergraduate at the time. Metzger's was the largest student bookstore in town. Their slogan, "You can get it at Metzger's," was also used in a sniggering way to refer to the single women who lived in the apartments above their store.

Labor Day weekend, Sy and I drove to Philadelphia to meet his parents, Fannie and Herman. They lived in a dangerous neighborhood, at the corner of Dauphin and Camac streets, where they ran a small neighborhood grocery store. Sy took me to stay overnight at his sister Sylvia's house in a neighborhood that was considered safer, and the next day, I met his parents. I had grown up in my family's grocery store, and I remember wanting to see their grocery store. I was so surprised to discover that their store was attached to their skinny, urban row house.

That weekend, much to my surprise, Sy asked me to marry him (deeply devoted to his parents, he had taken me home for his parents' approval). A bit like our first date, the effervescent Sy seemed

23

awkward and at a loss for words when he proposed. Unlike my own mother, who had opinions about everything and let them be known, Sy's mother was quiet to a fault. And in her eyes, because I loved her son, I could do no wrong.

We drove back to State College, and I started a Master's in the Speech Department, which included teaching Speech 200, a required general education course that exists to this day. I just loved teaching that course. About twenty years ago, a former student, Walter Pellish ('62), called me, out of the blue, to tell me that I was a person who changed his life in Speech 200. I felt ten feet tall at that moment. Here was this guy who had just been elected a county commissioner in West Virginia, and he marked the beginning of his career in public life to my course at Penn State. But my life as a budding Speech professor did not last long.

On January 31, 1954, I married Sy at the Manfield Ballroom, a kosher venue in Wilkes- Barre. His relatives arrived by charter bus from Philadelphia. Immigrants from Eastern Europe, they grew up in and around the city, depending on public transportation and never learning to drive.

We went to New York for a quick, weekend honeymoon, so I could get back to my teaching job. I refused to stay in the first room the New Yorker hotel gave us because it was too small.

"I'm on my honeymoon." I smiled to the man behind the front desk. "You must have a nicer room than this." They showed us to a room twice the size and brought us a bottle of champagne. I had little idea what champagne was at the time. I knew even less about sex or marriage.

My first miscarriage came not long after that weekend. In retrospect, it was probably a blessing, but at the time it was devastating. For some reason, Dr. Walter B. J. Scheyler, the local obstetrician, told me that if I did not keep my next pregnancy, I would not be able to have children. Sy and I had a frank discussion in which we decided that if we could not get pregnant, we would not adopt.

In 1956, Sy and I bought our first home, 325 Homan Avenue, on a wing and a prayer. It cost $26,500. We had a $20,000 mortgage from State College Federal Savings & Loan at four percent and a $5000 non-interest-bearing loan at $1,000 per month from M. L. Claster & Sons, a very loyal client of ours. They even allowed us a little wiggle room on a couple of those monthly payments.

After my second miscarriage, I didn't want to give up. I sought a specialist's help in Philadelphia, a doctor named Abraham Rakoff, who had known my sister's husband, Henry. Ultimately, Dr. Rakoff set me on the path to motherhood. Fertility treatment was very new at that time. Henry had been one of the key researchers in the field. The experimental treatment that ultimately helped me get pregnant involved substantial hormone therapy. I took my temperature every day; they "blew open" my fallopian tubes, and I made regular trips to Philadelphia to see Dr. Rakoff until I was safely pregnant again.

Thursday, October 16, 1958, a few days before my due date, I started having contractions early in the morning. I wanted to shower before I went to the hospital, but Sy wouldn't let me.

"You're just going to the hospital," he reminded me.

We arrived around 7 a.m., and our first daughter, Carol, was born around 7:00 that night. Against everyone's recommendation, I had attended the Penn State football game the weekend before, walking up many flights of stairs (Penn State beat Marquette, 40-8). Dr. Dale, my local doctor, was away, so the doctor on call, Dr. Paul Corman from Bellefonte, delivered the baby.

The nurse who helped me through the horrible labor, Gloria Saba, was the younger sister of someone I'd worked with at Padwe's Children's Shop in Wilkes-Barre. I had absolutely no idea what was happening and was so relieved to have someone else I knew in the delivery room. I found every aspect of pregnancy, giving birth, and parenting joyful but also stressful.

Though the culture said being a mother was supposed to come naturally, it did not come easily for me. Honestly, I didn't really start to like mothering until my children started talking, and I could have relationships with them through language. But we had climbed a huge mountain to get and stay pregnant, and Sy and I both felt extremely grateful for the gift that was our first daughter. The rest of my life, I felt the tug between work and family, something I think many women feel and which each of us learns to navigate in our own individual way.

CHAPTER 5
NOTHING HAPPENS UNTIL SOMEONE MAKES A SALE: THE BIRTH OF BARASH ADVERTISING

Almost as soon as I married Sy, he and Sid sent me out to sell. I sold things like the *Beaver Stadium Pictorial*, an early football program; the *Centre Democrat*, a weekly ad rag produced out of Bellefonte; and the *Pesticide Handbook*. I went out selling, no matter what the weather was like, no matter what they needed me to sell. Even when I was pregnant, I was out of the office bringing in revenue for our fledgling business. Sales was my jumpstart to personal growth.

Lesson #3: Everyone should experience the exhilarating highs and devastating lows that inevitably accompany in-person sales.

Though this was my first experience cold calling, you could say sales and scrappiness were in my blood, part of my upbringing and will to survive. My parents worked together in our grocery store, Capitol Grocery, in downtown Wilkes-Barre, two doors down from the Planter's Peanut Factory and showroom. Mr. Peanut walked up and down the street giving out samples.

My parents were quite entrepreneurial. One example: our store was the first to sell cut-up chicken in Wilkes-Barre. I would spend all afternoon, on a Saturday, cutting chickens into eight pieces in the back of our store. I think about it every time I eat chicken. We tried many little things that gave us an edge and brought us more customers. My mother's father was a peddler, who sold fabrics and notions from a cart he pulled around town. He knew absolutely everyone, even the people who didn't buy from him.

My parents sold Capitol Grocery in the late 1940s, and when my father became increasingly incapacitated from the complications of diabetes in the 1950s, my mother went out to work. Sy's parents worked together too. There was actually a lot more of that in the 1950s than most people think. But what made Sy and me different— really different—was that we very much ran our business as a team.

I can't remember a time when I didn't work. In college, I worked at least five different jobs to cover the parts of my tuition and living expenses not covered by my scholarships: I delivered the Sunday paper to the women's dorms; I worked in the catalog department of Pattee Library; and I ran the Sally's Snacks concession.

But selling for Sid and Sy was my first experience cold calling, learning how to stay organized, overcome objections, and see deals through to conclusion. I had to think about other people, not just myself. In marriage too, I had to learn how to be kinder and more considerate, aware of other people's feelings.

Lesson #4: In business relationships and personal relationships, focusing on others is not just important; it is crucial.

In all areas of life, I was getting off the bench and playing for real. It was exhilarating and very attractive to me.

On January 31, 1959, our fifth wedding anniversary, Sy was late. Sy was often late, and he was always late on our anniversary because he was working up to the last minute with our accountant preparing to submit our corporate taxes. On this anniversary, we purchased Nittany Ad-Ver-Tis-Er from Sid and Herman Friedman. They split up the Friedman and Barash clients between them, and that was the birth of Barash Advertising.

Sy, without my knowledge, started working on this deal in September, when I was pregnant. He didn't want to upset me near the end of my pregnancy, but on advice from our accountant, Ed Mittelman, who was also Sid's accountant, he had a hunch that Sid was interested in selling his half of their shared business.

"Offer him a price to buy or sell, and see what he says," Sy reported Mittelman saying, when he told me in November.

I believe his first offer was somewhere between $75,000 and $80,000. To pay the deposit, we borrowed $10,000 from People's Bank, using Sy's military insurance as collateral. Sid and his brother Herman held the rest of the note payable, and we paid them what was the going interest rate at that time. I wasn't always in the loop then, about the numbers side of the business. I think they held a note for $67,000 that we paid back a bit more than $1,000 monthly over five years for the billboard company.

We closed the deal on our fifth anniversary and moved the business to the basement of our house. I owned eight shares of the company; Sy owned eight shares, and we gave one to Sy's father to thank his parents for helping us get on our feet early in marriage.

We hired four employees: Edna Dombrowsky, our secretary; Robert Kelly, Art Director; Phyllis Bierly, who did ad layouts; and Frank Pontillo, bookkeeper. Edna and Phyllis worked for us for years, walking around the corner and through the backyards to get to our home office. We ran the company out of our basement until we bought an office downtown in 1967.

It was a tiny company, and we were all in the thick of things in that basement: Edna and I sat on the floor, rolling thousands of posters by hand; when we set up ads for our customers, I pulled the artwork on metal plates and sent them to the newspapers; and I took care of many of the invoices myself.

There were many weeks that we could not cash our own paychecks, and it often felt like the business was on the brink of collapse. But we always kept things moving forward, and the fact that both Sy and I loved sales—and often discussed and strategized sales as a team—was one key to our early success. Being the co-owner of that business, from the start, also meant that I was involved in decisions about how to build and grow the business, and how to ask banks and customers for money to finance that growth—something that many women over the years have told me is not easy for them.

1.

MARIAN "MIMI" BARASH

for

State College Borough Council

This I Believe . . .

Broad, long-range planning, including rapport and coordination with surrounding townships, looms as our most critical problem. It is imperative to (1) develop adequate standards and criteria to be equipped for the increasing number of zoning and annexation situations; (2) work toward hiring a trained borough planner who might work directly under the county planner and face our long-range problems objectively; (3) re-evaluate the manner in which we handle zoning changes and to have a more clearly defined method for making changes; (4) understand the role and projected growth of The University in order to keep pace with the demands that are our responsibility to meet.

I will sincerely

appreciate

your

SUPPORT

in the forthcoming

Election!

1. The brochure I took door-to-door when I was running for State College Borough Council.

2. In the 1960s we covered many different conferences and trade shows for our clients.

3. We created a themed booth and marketing program yearly for C-COR and Centre Video.

4. *Town & Gown* was still in its infancy when the Penn State humor magazine *Froth* parodied us.

4. FROWN & CLOWN

MARCH 1969

a froth parody   only 25c

THE 1960s

The 1960s were a time of big, risky moves in my life: Big risks in business, big financial risks to solidify the growing Jewish community in State College, and big personal risks as Sy became sick and I was forced to take on new responsibilities and learn new skills. Sy and I began the decade by taking a huge leap with our business: purchasing Morgan Signs in Altoona for $47,000, entirely on credit, when I was eight months pregnant with our second child. A month after we secured the loan, our daughter Nan was born on March 26, 1961.

Buying Morgan Signs meant expanding our reach, and that meant we had a bigger profile, and became a bigger threat. We would spend over a decade battling our much larger competitor, Mid-State Advertising, as they worked aggressively to run us out of business.

In 1960, Sy and I became the youngest charter members of the Jewish Community Center, the first synagogue in State College; we couldn't truly afford the money we contributed, but Sy was adamant that we needed to do it anyway.

In January 1966, starting to burst at the seams in our basement office, we made another move to expand into a new market, launching *Town & Gown*, a magazine with features about things to do in and around State College and Penn State. We had seen something similar in Cambridge, when we visited my brother, Sandy, during his freshman year at Harvard.

In 1967 we moved to our "office with the red door" downtown. It didn't really have a red door, but that's how people remembered the red trim. Soon after the move, we won some big contracts from the General State Authority of Pennsylvania through a political friend of my brother Sandy's, Bob Kunzig, who was head of the GSA and close to Richard Nixon.

Kunzig was a co-worker with Sandy, when Sandy interned with Hugh Scott in the U.S. Senate. John Heinz, at the time, was Senator Scott's legislative liaison, and Sandy lived with John. His girlfriend and later wife, Teresa, is now married to John Kerry. Heinz, a moderate Republican, was a really nice person, both to Sandy and to us. And Teresa Heinz was so nice to our mother that, at age seventy-seven, my mother worked door-to-door in Kingston to help get John Heinz elected the first time he ran for the Senate in 1976. Heinz later appointed me to the selection committee that nominated people for federal judgeships in the Philadelphia region, and I organized a fundraiser for him at the Nittany Lion Inn the night before he died in a plane crash in 1991.

There are some things that I look back and wonder, "Mimi, how in the hell did you do that?" In 1968, Congressman Dick Schweiker ('50), a classmate of Sy's from Penn State, threw his hat into the U.S. Senate race against Democratic incumbent Joe Clark. Schweiker set his sights on being introduced midfield at halftime in Beaver Stadium, as a Penn State alum to promote his candidacy for the U.S. Senate. Sy worked very hard for Schweiker's senatorial campaign and was at his best in that type of intense, one-on-one political work. I did all the heavy lifting behind the scenes to make the halftime introduction happen. We paid dearly for supporting Schweiker in a visible way with a drubbing in the local press the next day. We were registered Republicans in those days, but our hearts leaned liberal and, as Sy always told the children, "No one knows who you choose when you go in that little booth to vote."

***

During all this time, from 1956 to 1971, Eric Walker presided over the university as the community expanded dramatically on both sides of College Avenue. Student apartments sprang up everywhere, and a new wave of people—from outside the local community—moved into the area, investing in real estate, opening new businesses and shopping malls. The Penn State Board of Trustees became more diverse as well, with its first women and African-American trustees. I rode this wave onto the board, as an elected alumni trustee in 1976, my proudest service and deepest source of learning over a lifetime of engagement with Penn State.

In 1960, Beaver Field was dismantled from its original location near Rec Hall and moved to its current site on the east side of campus. The new, larger facility, renamed Beaver Stadium, was built up around the old field. Beaver Field held 30,000 people; the new stadium held 46,284. Long-time head football coach Rip Engel retired, and in 1966, Joe Paterno became the head coach of Penn State football. Penn State was a national leader in the implementation of Title IX and the rise of women's athletics, which opened up significant new opportunities for women at all levels of the university.

Innovation and entrepreneurship were always part of the Penn State magic, along with a socially progressive community spirit. The all-volunteer Park Forest Village Day Nursery School, a private preschool that took underprivileged children from throughout the county and still exists today, opened its doors in 1967.

The Art Alliance of Central Pennsylvania, wanting a "building of their own," purchased the Lemont Band Hall for $5,500 in 1968. The building was just a shell, and a group of local artists and business people worked together to turn it into an arts center. I co-chaired the effort to raise $30,000 to purchase and renovate the building with Bellefonte banker Mahlon Robb, who was in the room when we were given the loan to purchase Morgan Signs in 1961. In 2017, that same Art Alliance opened its own gallery in downtown State College.

In the 1960s, I was officially called "Mrs. Sy Barash," but looking back, I notice that I signed all my letters "Mimi Barash," a quiet, subtle feminism that would take root and grow later.

CHAPTER 6
WE'RE READY: GROWING OUR BUSINESS WITH MORGAN SIGNS

Adding Morgan Signs to our business was a huge, and terrifying, step. We were already leveraged to the hilt, but it made sense for us to purchase Morgan Signs to compete more effectively with Mid-State Advertising (later purchased by Pittsburgh Outdoor) in the Altoona market. We bought the business from Anthony Reck, who had purchased it five years earlier from General W. A. "Dick" Morgan and proceeded to run it into the ground.

We borrowed $32,000 from First Bellefonte Bank and Trust (now M & T). When we went to Bellefonte to close the loan with the bank officers, Harvey "Harv" Pearce and Mahlon Robb, I was dressed to the nines in a green and brown knit maternity suit.

That was the first time I was ever present during the borrowing of money. We had to bring our existing contract and lease books with us.

We got to the bank on Allegheny Street, and they opened the contract book. They rubber-stamped, "This account assigned to Bellefonte Bank and Trust" on every single one. In the middle of the meeting I started to cry.

"Does this mean that if something happens to Sy, you'll take everything?"

"No, we'll only take $32,000," Harv retorted.

"Okay. I can live with that," I said. And they went on stamping every single contract.

We borrowed the other $15,000 from Reck, who agreed to $5,000 per year, non-interest-bearing notes, payable at the end of 1963, 1964, and 1965, to finish the deal.

Blair County was the largest county in central Pennsylvania and densely populated with billboards owned or leased by our competition. By adding Morgan Signs, based in Blair County, we made ourselves a stronger force amidst larger rivals. Morgan gave us instant credibility. We were headquartered in State College, in Centre County. With the addition of Morgan Signs, our billboards now stretched across Centre, Blair, and eight contiguous counties: Bedford, Clearfield, Clinton, Huntingdon, Juniata, Mifflin, Snyder, and Union.

To grow faster, Sy approached General Morgan, the original owner of Morgan Signs, and asked for his help to rebuild and expand the business. Dick was a retired Brigadier General, who had enlisted out of high school and served in the army in World War I and World War II. He was widely known throughout the region, and his distinguished military service gave him additional credibility. We felt we had the opportunity to take General Morgan's contacts and experience and rejuvenate and expand the business he had founded. He agreed, and we worked closely together for more than a decade.

Dick was thin as a rail with a head of white hair, and he was a stickler. He lived in Altoona and would drive around at night, making certain the lights were working on all of our signs. Over seventy years old, he would go back during the day and go up on a ladder to change the bulbs himself, if necessary.

Morgan's signs were of many different sizes, and all of them were hand-painted, mostly on wood. We were already moving toward the industry standard of that time, posters that were pre-printed and posted on metal structures, but we still needed painters. Soon after we purchased Morgan Signs, we approached Joe Mack, an African-American graduate student in Graphic Arts at Penn State, and offered him a job as our sign painter. We sent Joe to paint the front of Jack Wilkinson's store in Bellefonte. Jack was a close friend and business advisor.

The next time we saw Jack he said, "Are you sure you want to do this? Are you sure the area is ready for this?"

Sy said, "If they're not ready, they'll have to get ready."

Even Joe himself had said to us when we offered him the job, "Are you sure your customers are ready for me?"

And Sy said, "*We're* ready." Joe was a brilliant sign painter and became a friend as well. He painted vivid murals on the walls of our basement office that reminded me of him long after he'd moved on from State College.

From the moment we purchased Morgan Signs, Mid-State Advertising was a thorn in our side, working to destroy our business and make themselves even stronger in Altoona and Blair County. The owner, Henry Posner, became a real bully. Mid-State reps called our customers and tried to get our leases out from under us.

"They said, 'We'll pay you double,'" our shop landlord in Altoona, Lou Leopold, reported back to us after they called on him. Lou had a high, squeaky voice. You wouldn't know he was a man if you only heard him on the phone. "Mimi, what's going on? This guy just called us and offered us twice what you're paying, for those locations."

Sy and I went to Blank Rome, a law firm in Philadelphia, because Edwin P. Rome was a lawyer who had won a case for an independent theater that was getting pushed out of downtown Philadelphia by Warner Brothers.

"You can't afford me," Rome said. But he told us to contact the U.S. Attorney's office and explained how to get a cease-and-desist order under U.S. antitrust statutes. I copied hundreds of pages on a Nord liquid copier, documenting how Pittsburgh Outdoor, the larger company, had been using unfair and illegal practices to put Morgan Signs, a tiny company by comparison, out of business. At that time, to make copies, you had to put two pieces of paper—one negative and one positive—through a wet solution that was smelly and took a very long time.

Sy delivered the pile of papers to the U.S. Attorney's office in Pittsburgh to register our complaint. As luck would have it, Joe Ammerman ('50), the U.S. Attorney for the Western District of Pennsylvania at that time, was a business acquaintance. He came to our basement office personally to follow up on our letter and determine if it was worthy of further attention. He ordered a full-scale investigation, and ultimately Pittsburgh Outdoor received a stiff fine and for several years had to operate under close scrutiny from the U.S. Attorney's office. Most of what we knew about the investigation, at the time, came from Sidney Tobin, who had already sold a company similar to ours to Pittsburgh Outdoor.

"Life is tough in Pittsburgh," he reported, speaking in code about the fines and oversight by the U.S. Attorney's office.

I never met Henry Posner. Later, in the 1980s and '90s, Pittsburgh Outdoor (by then they had been acquired by Penn Advertising, which was later acquired by Lamar) tried to buy me out many times, but I refused to sell to them. I felt their offers were low-ball, and they did not take me seriously as a business person, in part because I was a woman. In the end, I was smart to hold out, keep growing my business, and sell to Lamar directly more than twenty years later.

CHAPTER 7

REMEMBER WHERE YOU COME FROM: JEWISH LIFE IN HAPPY VALLEY

I came from a kosher home in a tightly knit, small-town Jewish community. My mother faithfully made Shabbat dinner every Friday night, complete with blessings over candles and bread. For some reason, we skipped the blessing over wine, and the only times I ever saw liquor in our house growing up were after funerals or on Passover.

Temple Israel in Wilkes-Barre, where my parents were founding members, appealed to conservative, middle-of-the-roaders in Jewish tradition. Most of my extracurricular activities centered around the Jewish Community Center, where I spent most weekends, and occasionally after-school activities. Hebrew School at Temple Israel was mandatory and came before all other after school activities.

When I arrived in State College, there was significantly less Jewish energy and observance than I'd experienced as a child. There was no local synagogue in State College, although several of the surrounding communities—Clearfield, Philipsburg, Lewistown, Lock Haven, and Huntingdon—had their own buildings and rabbis. The country clubs in State College and Bellefonte still did not accept Jewish or African American members, and there was very little talk about religion in the local community. Both on and off campus, the mainstream was Christian and, in terms of Jewish activity and identity, I kept my religious observance mostly to myself in those days.

Though we were quietly Jewish, it was very important to Sy and me that State College be a place where Jewish traditions would be observed and passed on to the next generation. We invested time and money into the local Jewish community long before we were financially secure ourselves.

Lesson #5: Staying true to what is important to you is essential to your wellness and happiness. Some things don't deserve stinginess.

Friday night services and High Holiday (Rosh Hashanah and Yom Kippur) services for Jewish students took place at Hillel, a cultural organization for Jewish students, above Temple Market (now Green Bowl) on West Beaver Avenue. The three Jewish sororities and seven Jewish fraternities took turns sponsoring Friday night services and ensuring that students walked the mile or so off campus to Hillel. In 1954, a group of faculty and townspeople formed the Jewish Community Council of State College and Bellefonte, and as the Penn State faculty grew rapidly in the 1960s, the Jewish community expanded and became more diverse.

Though there was, and still is, a Jewish cemetery in Bellefonte, in 1957, a group of State College residents wanted to establish a Jewish cemetery closer to State College. The group was led by local merchant and philanthropist Charles Schlow, whose first wife, Bella, was ill with breast cancer. By then Hillel had moved to Locust Lane. As more and more Jewish people moved into the community, Hillel became the de facto congregation for Jewish families in State College. A special meeting of the Jewish Community Council met at Hillel and passed a resolution to reserve a "traditional Jewish" section in Centre County Memorial Park on Benner Pike. They needed eighteen families to commit to being buried in the cemetery, and Sy secured us, at ages 24 and 31, two cemetery plots.

The original "Jewish section" of Centre County Memorial Park observed all the rules of orthodox Jewish burial. Sy was buried there in 1975, and someday I will go there as well. However, the State College Jewish community, overall, was quite diverse and liberal, and people practiced their Judaism in many different ways. In 1984, the Jewish community opened a second section of the cemetery that allowed for spouses and children of inter-marriage.

The drive for a synagogue of our own took root in those years, a place that would be not only a house of worship, but also a place to hold Sunday School and religious school for our children, and a hub of community service and engagement. In the early 1960s, when Jewish townspeople wanted to purchase land for our synagogue, Sy and I were the youngest charter members. Nathan Krauss, the token Jewish member of the People's National Bank board, got us a special rate of four percent to borrow the money.

When Sy explained the deal he'd agreed to without asking me, I was livid.

"Sy, we're acting like big shots. We don't have the money." My voice got louder, "Why in the world did you do that?"

"Sometimes, when it's the right thing, you just have to do it," he calmly reminded me. He just kept saying, "We're gonna do it. We have to do it. There is no choice." And ultimately, I came to see that he was right.

That conversation was typical of Sy and of our relationship: he got his way by stating his opinions as if they were facts. And then he moved on. I was angry for days, but ultimately came to respect his decisions and accept them. I still get great pleasure stretching my capacity for philanthropy to help do the right thing, even when I feel I can't quite "afford" it.

***

It took another five years to raise the money and build the small synagogue, which opened in 1965. For the first twenty years, the synagogue was not affiliated with Orthodox, Conservative, or Reform Judaism.

Because State College had such a diverse Jewish community, one that was small compared to the Christian world around us, the rabbi played a key role, both holding us together and interacting with the broader community. This enabled us to form alliances, such as with the Interfaith Mission, and to collaborate with other groups to help remove the remaining barriers to religious freedom. Anti-Semitism occasionally reared its head on and off campus, but in general we all somehow managed to get along. Still, the recent painting of swastikas on the garbage containers behind a mostly Jewish fraternity, Beta Sigma Beta, reminds us that the work of community building, across our differences, is never done.

I believe one unusual facet of the success of the State College Jewish community grows from the leadership and tenacity of individuals who have chosen to convert to Judaism. We are all better for having shared their experience of chosen faith and for learning from one another's stories and beliefs.

Everyone eats "Jewish" in State College now—you can enjoy a lox and bagel at Irving's, and soon, they predict, we might have a kosher deli in the new Hillel at the intersection of Garner Street and Beaver Avenue. In 2013, the congregation completed an endowment campaign of nearly $3 million to ensure the future of our Jewish traditions, hopefully into perpetuity. In the 1960s, we were living through a time when all of this seemed remote but possible, and we felt it was our responsibility to take the lead in building a strong and enduring Jewish community in and around State College.

CHAPTER 8
LEARNING TO ASK FOR HELP: THE SUMMER OF 1963

One of the tougher phone calls I ever fielded came in the summer of 1963. Sy had a cluster of unusual symptoms: he was very tired, lacked appetite, and his skin was an unusual color. He was eventually diagnosed with hepatitis, and he spent most of that summer in bed. This required that I put on many of his sales and customer relationship hats, in and out of the office, along with my role preparing work for our customers. This was the first of many instances in which Sy's illness presented me with new opportunities to flex my business muscles with our clients, my husband, and myself.

Lesson #6: Moving out of your comfort zone allows for greater possibilities—and often requires asking other people to help.

Because Sy ran the out-of-office parts of our business, and I ran the in-house parts, I didn't know Phil Sieg and had never spoken with him when I picked up the phone that afternoon. Sy had told me about Phil, and his business partner, Alex Gregory ('49), was our backyard neighbor. Phil and Alex were developing Holiday Inns (now the Ramada) in State College and Altoona, as well as their planned-community development of Toftrees in Patton Township. They were a very new client of ours when Sy came down with hepatitis.

Phil was calling to complain, "What's taking you so long to secure that location for us?" He was referring to a location to erect a new outdoor billboard structure near the Wye intersection in Duncansville that was clearly visible to Altoona-bound traffic.

My first thought was to say some version of, "Sy is sick…" but I intuitively knew that excuses would not fly.

"Let me explore the problem," I said, wondering what he was really talking about. "I'll report back to you in a week."

When I heard Sy walking around, I went upstairs to find out the details. Sy shook his head.

"I can't even get to first base with them." He was referring to the Pennsylvania Railroad local operators who had given him a runaround and then, finally, referred him to the regional office in Buffalo, New York. Sy had asked General Morgan, who had close ties with Pennsylvania Railroad folks locally, to follow-up, but hadn't heard back.

I tracked down General Morgan to determine where we stood.

"Not too promising, Mimi," Dick told me kindly. I asked him to find out who was the person in Buffalo who could get this past where it was stuck. I felt strongly, based on my conversation with Phil, that if we didn't secure that specific location, we'd lose the whole Holiday Inn contract for multiple billboards in Blair and Centre Counties. None of our competitors had any signs on the Pennsylvania Railroad property they coveted, so this was a chance to stay ahead of our competition. My debating temperament piqued both my fighting spirit and my confidence, and I kicked into high gear.

Dick referred me to a guy by the name of Jerry Berner, who was in charge of all railroad real estate throughout the northeast. It took me a few tries to get Jerry to return my call, during which time I researched the problem from different angles, as I would have done preparing for a debate. Because I've always believed in a down-to-earth, direct approach to things that matter most, I engaged Jerry in the story of how Sy first got a rash called purpura and was hospitalized, and that now he had come down with hepatitis and been confined to bed.

"I'm trying to be the glue to keep things together," I said, "with little experience to solve this problem." I gathered courage. "Jerry, you're the one person who can help me do that."

He answered slowly, choosing his words carefully. "Well, historically, we've had a policy against leasing to billboard companies on this property," he began. I could hear him tapping his pen, as he added, "This is for safety and visibility in both directions."

"What might make it something you could do for the first time?" I asked, almost as if I was talking to myself, and then I started brainstorming out loud. "What if we adapted the size to smaller than the standard 30-sheet? That way," I said, "we can ensure there are no obstacles to visibility for the trains traveling in either direction." As I thought this through out loud with him, I put our scrappiness and flexibility to advantage. If we were in a secret bidding war with Mid-State Outdoor on this one, they would be unlikely to deviate from standard sizes.

"Let me talk to my team, and I'll get back to you. It might be a good time to revisit this policy." I sensed an opening with his words. "But it may take some time."

"I appreciate your willingness to examine it. It sounds like you are inclined to change the policy. Am I reading you correctly?"

"No guarantees. But we'll discuss it." About four weeks later, we consummated a ten-year lease with the Pennsylvania Railroad, the cornerstone of our much larger deal with Phil Sieg and Alex Gregory's corporate entity, Federated Home & Mortgage. Federated remained one of our strong, loyal, growing customers through many decades. And Phil Sieg became an important business advisor and friend to me after Sy died, through projects as well as losses we shared together. Over many years, I learned a lot from him about how to make sound business decisions, under the most challenging of circumstances.

With the Wye intersection, I felt I had created a solution that took everyone's interests into account, in a tasteful way that also protected the land owned by the railroad.

CHAPTER 9
MAKE WAY FOR BIG IDEAS: THE BIRTH OF THE ARTS
FESTIVAL

When our office was in the basement of our home, there was no getting away from the business. Fights about the business between Sy and me often festered for long periods of time. Sy was full of big ideas, lots of them. I was much more pragmatic and methodical, focused on making money. When Sy got angry, which happened rarely, he moved on quickly. It was much harder for me to let go and move on, especially when I thought I was right.

If I had to leave the house just to cool my mind, it was as if I was running away from the family, not just getting some perspective on a disagreement about the business with the man who was both my husband and my business partner. To prevent conflicts, Sy and I decided to separate our offices in the new building downtown, with me on the first floor and Sy upstairs. And, for the first time, each of us had our own assistant.

I remember when local artist Dee Blumenthal came to see Sy and me about her big idea: we met in Sy's office on the second floor, which was always strewn with piles and piles of papers. Dee was fabulously creative; she moved quickly and intensely in everything she did. Her paintings were bright, large, and abstract. Her work drew me into something very profound, the same swirl of passion and rebellion I sensed in my sister Sylvia's paintings. I don't think I connected the dots at the time, but for many women artists in the 1960s, there were tiny new openings for expression, but also decades, even centuries, of oppression to overcome in getting to that place of public expression.

"The Pennsylvania Council of the Arts is giving grants of $2000 to communities to start local arts festivals," Dee began. "This is a good idea for State College. We have the creative people and the kind of community that could put this together. If Altoona can do it, we certainly can. We *should* do it. I want your help."

Sy stood up behind his desk, as if he was stepping into action. We both loved art—graphic arts and performing arts—and agreed with Dee that the combination of practicing artists in the local community and burgeoning interest in Fine Art and Performing Art as legitimate disciplines at the university made State College a great place to launch a local arts festival.

Lesson #7: Sometimes, when it's the right time, people who don't usually work together see the same thing, and a big new idea is possible.

Early on, State College Chamber of Commerce president Wally Lloyd ('49), a leader at Cannon Instruments, endorsed the idea, giving it instant stature and credibility in the local business community. Jules Heller, the Dean of Arts of Architecture and a nationally recognized printmaker, also believed in the potential to create something that could turn our sleepy town into a summer destination. We offered free billboards to advertise the Festival, but Dean Heller was opposed to billboards, even if they were free.

Before we knew it, a new alliance was formed. Volunteers and leaders from the business and arts communities snapped into action together, supporting the idea and making it happen that first year on a miniscule budget.

"The Festival" epitomizes the power of passionate people to plan and execute vital local projects, with minimum paid staff, through the work of hundreds of dedicated volunteers. We jumped many hurdles along the way to arrive at the fifty-year celebration in 2016, and I laugh when I think back on that first Arts Festival, which was a real free-for-all.

Artists displayed their art along a snow fence on College Avenue in front of Old Main. The artists who came early claimed their spots and set up their wares. Bill Coleman ('49), the portrait photographer for our sorority composite—girls reported he had "Roman hands and Russian fingers," which would now be considered sexual harassment—showed up early in the morning and grabbed the best position to sell his Amish photographs.

The next year, with much pomp and circumstance, Governor Ray Shafer landed in a helicopter on the grass in front of Old Main to kick off the Festival. President Walker arranged for Sy to meet with the governor, personally, to ask him for this favor, and a decade later, the former governor paid a surprise visit to Sy when he was in Memorial Sloan Kettering Cancer Center in New York.

In the early years, I worked behind the scenes while Sy was extremely active in making sure the Arts Festival connected the campus and the community. To make it more of a shared event, planners placed the main stage for Festival performances on the lawn in front of Old Main; they moved the artists' booths onto the campus; and they secured the closure of Allen Street for entertainment. The university and scores of local businesses contributed financially and with in-kind services, providing the sense of a big, shared community celebration. Year by year, the Festival became the thing to do for four days every July, drawing people from all across Pennsylvania and beyond.

As the Festival grew, many local artists got their start there. Spectra Wood founders Larry and Rita Roeshot, both ('57), started selling cutting boards at the first Festival. Spectra Wood grew into a thriving local manufacturer, now in a 100,000 square foot facility with over $10 million annual revenue and 125 employees. Others, like woodworker Phil Sollman ('71) and his wife, medallic sculptor Jeanne Stevens-Sollman ('72), became nationally recognized and gained major commissions for their work based on contacts made through the Festival.

We were truly off and running by 1975. By then, the tenth Festival, a new dean, Walter Walters, and a new Penn State University President, John W. Oswald, joined as loyal supporters. I especially remember that tenth Festival because the board dedicated it to the memory of my husband Sy, who lost his two-year and two-month battle with lung cancer on February 8, 1975, at age forty-eight.

To be on the Festival board, then and now, was both an honor and a privilege. In the late 1990s, the Festival asked me to serve as president of the board. Having been elected in 1991 as the first female chair of Penn State's Board of Trustees, I strived to strengthen the "town-gown" relationship to benefit the Arts Festival and the community.

I'm reminded of the Festival every day, as my home is filled with treasures I've acquired over the years: everything from large-scale graphic art and sculpture to handmade baskets and special, one-of-a-kind clothing and jewelry.

My heart beats with special pride for what this collective community has created, one of the many reminders of how work in the community pays back, again and again, and of so many wonderful local people who worked hard and overcame roadblocks to create something that is larger than any of us could do alone.

CHAPTER 10
EMPLOYEES ARE YOUR BUSINESS: THE MASS EXODUS

After seven years running our business in a zoned residential neighborhood from the basement of our home at 325 Homan Avenue, we bought and remodeled a fraternity house at the corner of South Allen Street and East Nittany Avenue downtown and made it our office. At that point, the business was made up of Barash Advertising and Morgan Signs, and we had about twenty employees between the agency and the billboard shop in Altoona.

Our visibility grew steadily, and new clients began knocking on what everyone called "the red door." That splash of color made a big statement in our small, monochromatic town.

The move took careful planning, as well as more borrowed money and hard work on everyone's part so that we didn't miss a beat in delivering service to our growing customer base, including M. L. Claster & Sons, our anchor client, for whom we produced all of their advertising each week. All of us, Sy and I and all our key employees, were quite exhausted both from the move and from the demands of our growing clientele.

I first got a hint something strange was happening when I went down to the new office on a Sunday, while the girls were at Sunday School, to pick up some papers I needed to work on at home after our Sunday night bowling league. From all those years with the office in the basement, I was used to working at my kitchen table and on our living room couch, and I preferred to work at home late at night and over the weekends.

When I walked in, the lights were already on, and Walt Gilbride, an account executive at Barash Advertising, was busy cleaning out his desk. He looked flustered when he saw me, and he started pushing things together. He quickly closed the top file. At first it wasn't so surprising: when you're the boss and you walk in, and someone is doing something personal, they close it up. It's just like someone closing their laptop suddenly today.

"What brings you here on a Sunday?" I asked cheerfully, moving into his office.

"Just cleaning up," he said, never looking up.

They walked out the next week, all three of them together: Walt Gilbride, Account Executive of Barash Advertising; Bob Kelley, Art Director; and another artist whose name I've forgotten. When they left, they took a couple of clients with them, including the Community Bank of Port Matilda, who also loaned them money to start their business.

I remember the exit as ugly. They scheduled it right before *Town & Gown* was due at the printers, and before Sy and I were scheduled to take the girls on a much-needed summer vacation to the Expo '67 World's Fair in Montreal.

Racing to finish and get out of town, we put an abstract shape on the cover of the July 1967 *Town & Gown* because we had no one on staff who could design a new cover. We had one other artist, at the time, who was very loyal but with little experience, so we needed to find two people very quickly.

Replacing employees took weeks or even months back then: placing ads, reading resumes, checking references. Through a friend, we found a temporary substitute, a very religious man who was an artist at the university. He helped us out part-time while we took our two-week family vacation and then came back to search for real replacements. There were no computers or mobile phones then. It was landlines only. But, somehow, we survived and so did our business.

I can still see Bob Kelley ('63) with his black cape and greasy black hair, sometimes pulled back in a ponytail. He was tall and temperamental, full of big ideas, many of which we couldn't begin to implement. He made fancy birthday hats for the girls out of cut paper. He pushed all of us to try new colors, new designs, new types of pens, and photography. And for some reason, he hated the electric company. One month when he was paying his electric bill, he carefully took his Xacto knife and cut out extra little rectangles on his bill before putting it back in the envelope with his check.

"That will fix those bastards," he whispered under his breath.

Over the years there were many incidents with employees that totally shocked me. Once, our head sign-painter stole from us. He was using our supplies to do his own work on the side. We also employed his brother, and we had to fire both of them.

I found it very difficult to understand moves like this. We attempted to instill a sense of teamwork and family among our employees. We paid well for the market; we covered one hundred percent of our employees' health insurance and bought cars for our sales people. We brought in food when people had to work late, and we threw the best holiday parties in town, including gifts for all our employees' children.

But sometimes, none of that was enough, and we lost key people—especially to the university, who could provide a significant discount on employees' and their children's education. It took time and effort to replace experienced, qualified personnel.

I took it hard and personally and often found myself asking, "What could I have done better?"

During Sy's, lifetime he managed all the employee relationships. I felt he was much better at it than me, because he was more capable of understanding the other person's point of view. For me, at that time, I was (and still am) a person with a great need to be appreciated. In hindsight I see how that need to be appreciated inhibited my capacity to see things from the other person's point of view. This was particularly true of my employees.

As I get older and reflect on how I might have done things differently, I see where I was too quick to anger and disappointment, and less attentive to each employee's personal needs and individual style. Now I see nothing wrong with someone dressing in their own style at work, but for a long time, it was really important that all our employees looked and acted a certain way. And I still have trouble setting aside, in a work context, what seems to be untraditional behavior.

Especially when Sy was sick and after he died, I felt everyone was looking to me for leadership. I think there were some people who couldn't stand the idea of a woman boss. But there were also flaws in my leadership. When three of your key people leave together, there's a message. But I didn't stop to think about it at the time. I was so frightened and working so hard for what felt like survival, I rarely considered the emotional side of the business. Under stress, I tended to perceive our key employees as competing with me. It became about me vs. them, not about us, and that often limited their ability to thrive.

Lesson #8: In business, be sure to engage your leadership team. Involve them in big decisions. Honor and nurture their individual spirits.

CHAPTER 11
GIVE OTHER PEOPLE ROOM TO GROW: WITT YEAGLEY RETURNS HOME

In February 1969, when *Town & Gown* was in its infancy, Witt Yeagley ('50) became the magazine's first full-time staff member. He treated the magazine as his own, shaping it into a publication that became extremely popular with its readers. Starting as Managing Editor and Sales Manager, Witt served us and the community over forty years, in every capacity.

Sy and Witt were students together at Penn State. Witt grew up and stayed in State College after graduation. He opened a Spudnut franchise that became so successful the company moved him to California to manage their regional office. Witt's father, Henry Yeagley, had been a professor of Physics at Penn State, and Witt was keen to return to his hometown. After Spudnut, he moved on to a sales position at Reeves Hoffman, a manufacturer in Carlisle.

Witt approached Sy to talk about his ideas for growing *Town & Gown,* and Sy offered him a job, for the whopping salary of $10,200 a year. Witt was intensely in love with State College and Penn State. In addition to improving production and cutting costs, Witt hired experienced local writers and historians, such as Jo Chesworth ('60) and Lee Stout ('69), and began including at least one feature about local history in each issue. At the time, no one else was writing about the region's history, and so our magazine became an important voice of change and progress. Witt worked with mayor Jo Hays to highlight ordinary people's enduring contributions to the community.

Our early reader surveys suggested that both townspeople and visitors were most interested in the history of State College and Penn State and, after that, profiles of interesting people, living or dead.

Because about thirty percent of the area population turns over each year, the magazine played a role in welcoming newcomers.

A student once wrote to us, "It makes me feel like I belong."

Early on, I had tried to use *Town & Gown* as a platform for my own points of view, as I had done as a student editor for the *Collegian*, with a new monthly column called "Catalyst." After I published an article protesting the Elks Club's refusal to admit African-American members, a group of advertisers, encouraged by a business person who was active in the Elks Club, threatened to boycott *Town & Gown*, and I quickly stopped using the magazine as my pulpit. I trusted Witt and gave him free rein to make *Town & Gown* the magazine it still is today.

Witt's approach was to use local history, current events, and inspiring everyday citizens to connect *Town & Gown* with the emotional heart of Happy Valley. In 1973, when Joe Paterno was offered the job as head coach of the New England Patriots, Witt decided to stop the presses, change the cover, and feature Paterno on the cover. He used *Town & Gown* as the centerpiece of a campaign that urged, "Joe, Don't Go Pro." We included postcards of the cover inside the magazine, and we also placed them at high traffic destinations throughout the Centre region, encouraging people to mail them to Joe with their comments. Thousands of people responded, and Joe turned down the Patriots. Years later, Joe said in conversation with me that the promotion played a role in his final decision to make Penn State his family's home forever.

Witt was prematurely gray and looked older than he was. He helped many people in many quiet ways, and grew *Town & Gown* as a vehicle for community service. For example, he was an advocate of the American Red Cross. Every month there was an ad in *Town & Gown* recognizing people who reached milestones in donating blood, and he sold a long-term sponsorship to the Autoport. Witt was a persistent salesman and had a loyal family of advertisers. He was very understated and smart; I could always count on him to get things done. The people who reported to him found him a real stickler for details, and sometimes I found him a bit ornery. Every time he bothered me, I'd take a pin from my pin cushion, pull it out, and put it somewhere else in the pin cushion. But I always felt he and I respected one another and worked well as a team.

One of the bigger disagreements I had with Witt was in 1991 when the Arts Festival requested competitive bids to produce the official *Festival Guide*. Festival volunteers had always produced the *Guide* internally. It took a huge amount of volunteer effort, and they could never break even on it. So Linda Gall and Phil Walz, the president and executive director of the Festival, made a decision to outsource the program.

Witt was opposed to our bidding on the project. He felt it would sidetrack us, and that it could undermine our capacity to grow the core *Town & Gown* product. I saw it differently: as an opportunity to develop another revenue stream, using the team we already had to generate additional revenue without increased overhead. Additionally, I saw it as a project that would give our designers and salespeople another venue to explore their creativity. The Arts Festival was obviously growing dramatically, and I saw a way to grow along with them, while solving a big headache for them.

Witt felt he was right, and I felt I was right.

Lesson #9: The best way to come to a decision is sometimes to hear the objections.

But it was one of those cases where there was no way to meet in the middle, and I insisted that Witt work with me on the proposal. We bid on it, were the successful bidder, and we've been publishing the *Festival Guide* ever since, contributing more than $300,000 additional revenue to the Festival to date.

The Festival Guide was both comprehensive and beautiful, and underscored our capacity to produce high-quality print magazines. It's been recognized nationally as a model of arts programming publications. The fact that we could make it available free was a real bonus. Plus, we took something that had been a monkey on the Festival's back and turned it into a major source of revenue for them. It was a collaborative project that revealed the power of the *Town & Gown* brand. It is also an example of a time I saw something that others didn't see, but in order to seize the opportunity I had to pull rank and inspire my team to make it happen for the first time. I guess I can be a bit ornery, too!

CHAPTER 12
LEARNING TO LAUGH AT MYSELF: *FROWN & CLOWN*

Sy and I were driving East on College Avenue (it was two lanes then) in our Plymouth sedan, about to turn right on South Allen and go out to lunch at McLanahan's Drug Store (now the location of Amazon), where we would mingle and schmooze at the counter with other small business owners: Joe Hurvitz ('38) of Hur's Men's Shop, Al ('43) and Sam ('41) Crabtree of Crabtree's Jewelers, Bill and Arnold ('31) Kalin of Kalin's, Jack Harper ('22) of Harper's, Charlie Levine ('30) of Levine's, and others.

Much to our surprise, we observed several well-dressed male students hawking a six-by-nine-inch black-and-white magazine resembling *Town & Gown*. Coincidentally, they were members of Beta Sigma Rho, Sy's fraternity. We stopped before the turn; I rolled down my window and paid twenty-five cents for my copy. I couldn't decide whether to laugh or cry. It was called *Frown & Clown*, and it looked exactly like my beloved third child, *Town & Gown*.

Sy was familiar with *Froth*, the Penn State humor magazine founded in 1909, from his undergraduate days. When Sy returned to Penn State after World War II, *Froth* was one of his extra-curricular activities. In their senior year together, Sy was the business manager, and Sam Vaughan ('51), who later became the Editor in Chief of Doubleday, the editor. Sy and I met up with Sam and his wife Josie at the "Horseshoe Bar" (then Vazacs, now 7B) on our honeymoon to New York City. *Froth* had to go underground for several years in the early 1960s, when the university administration deemed their radical racial and sexual content "vulgar and offensive."

Once a year *Froth* parodied a national publication. I had never paid much attention to *Froth*. It turned me off because fraternity men controlled both the business and editorial sides. But it got my attention on that random day in March 1969. *Town & Gown*, just three years old, had sixteen black-and-white pages and very little in the way of unique, in-depth content. We were still a little magazine where you could find out what was going on in the mostly sleepy Happy Valley. To be recognized at all, especially by students who were not our target audience, energized me to pursue higher quality and more in-depth editorial content. Their mockery of my monthly opinion column, "Catalyst," made me laugh. They signed it "M.U.D.", instead of my byline, "m.u.b."

Lesson #10: Parody is a kind of flattery. Attention on a higher level means that you're gaining a following.

It meant we were taken seriously enough to be the butt of a shared joke. The *Froth* parody issue created a buzz in the community and served for months as a conversation starter. We used it as an opportunity to pursue a new line of advertisers, those who wanted to reach students as well as townspeople and visitors.

***

Flash forward to July 1983 at that same corner of College Avenue and Allen Street, when I ran into another surprise: *State College Magazine* launched during the Central Pennsylvania Festival of the Arts. It was full standard magazine size, four-color throughout, published by our advertising agency competitor, Snavely Associates. This one I took very seriously, especially its cover featuring my friend and client Jim Palmer.

Lesson #11: There is always competition; you either continue to get better at what you do, or you pass into oblivion.

We immediately determined to go from black-plus-one-color to four-color, while working to increase the number of pages with the type of in-depth, local, and historical content our readers preferred. *Town & Gown* celebrated its fiftieth anniversary with the largest issue ever in January 2016; by then I had been serving as a part-time consultant to *Town & Gown*'s new owners since 2008.

Town & Gown is a story of survival and continuing to do

something I love—and I believe the community needs—even when it's not the most profitable part of my overall business. That fiftieth anniversary edition received the Arnold Addison Award from the State College Borough Council, in recognition of outstanding contributions to improving the quality of life and promoting relations between Penn State and the Borough of State College. This is what I always dreamed of: a magazine that would create for the larger community the kinds of connections between people and events at Penn State and in State College that had made my own life so fruitful.

1. And while Sy was fighting cancer, I became a much more visible presence between State College and Penn State.

2. Soon after Sy's cancer diagnosis, we created an ROTC award to honor General Dick Morgan, who helped us grow our billboard business.

3. The living room of our home was my second office for much of the 1970s.

4. The day that Jesse Owens came to C-COR to launch the Olympic series of amplifiers.

5. Nan and Carol at Carol's high school graduation in 1976.

6. Joe Paterno said that our "Don't Go Pro, Joe" campaign influenced his family's decision to stay in State College.

THE 1970s

There was very little that didn't break open for me in the 1970s. In 1970 I turned thirty-seven. My husband, Sy, was forty-three, and our daughters, Carol and Nan, were eleven and eight. Nixon was president, and our troops were still deep into the war in Vietnam. Watergate was around the corner driving permanent changes in our country's trust in the presidency.

It really was the dawning of the Age of Aquarius in the Centre Region, including State College borough and the five townships surrounding it. There was attention to the arts, environmental activism, and profound new opportunities for women, African-Americans, and other minorities in the community. In the 1970s, due to circumstances I could never have anticipated and probably would have rejected if they'd been offered to me, I became a recognized force of change in the State College community for the first time.

In our business, we bought the first IBM typesetting machine in the region, enabling us to bring typesetting in-house and gain the capacity to prepare artwork we previously had to outsource. This technology breakthrough transformed the preparation of commercial art, ultimately allowing us to press a button and send work directly to print, eliminating the smell of rubber cement and all the intermediaries we previously had to pay to get our creative work out into the world.

In 1970, Jack Oswald became the thirteenth president of Penn State. Because of student unrest, the president's home was moved off campus to Boalsburg. Oswald arrived with a heavily involved wife, Rose, an executive administrator, Doris Seward, and an absolutely delightful mother-in-law, Blossom Owens. Under Oswald's leadership, Penn State grew to become a regional and national powerhouse academically as well as culturally. The university opened its first art museum in 1972, next to the original Creamery.

Sy suggested that the chamber of commerce hold a welcoming event for the new president. The reception was originally scheduled for the Elks Club, which at that time would not consider African-American people for membership.

Charles T. Davis, a professor of English and the first African-American professor to receive tenure at Penn State (in 1960), called me one afternoon.

"I'm not calling to complain," he said, "but I think it sends the wrong message to have the official welcome at a place where not all people are welcome."

I thanked him for his concern and immediately tracked down Sy, who was on the road in Middleburg, in Snyder County, servicing a billboard client. I told him about the call from Davis and my instinct that he was correct.

"I agree with you," Sy said. "It has to be changed."

In those days, Sy was the public face of our big ideas; I was the person who did the work behind the scenes to make things happen. I quickly found another place, the Nittany Lion Inn, to host the event, and called Chuck Mong, executive director of the chamber of commerce, to propose the change to him. On my own, I would have just gone ahead and changed the venue, because it was "the right thing to do," but Sy insisted, correctly, that I get the committee behind us to avoid offending anyone or leaving anyone out of the process—and so he and I wouldn't be left alone, hanging out to dry with the decision to boycott the Elks Club.

That dinner served as a big turning point in the community around issues related to equality and diversity. I have letters from many local leaders, including Professor Charles Davis, thanking us for adding our voices to this issue. Looking back, I can see how that event put Mimi and Sy, together, for the first time, on the front lines of much broader moves to make State College and Penn State more inclusive for all people.

Our visibility from the welcome event and Oswald's close friendship with Sy opened up many other doors for us. At Oswald's request, Sy took on leadership of the local American Heart Association fundraising and PR efforts.

At the start of 1972, for the first time in our thirteen years of business together as a couple, Sy and I were able to pay ourselves on time, and we had a steady book of business we could count on month to month. But all of that was about to change.

***

In June, 1972, Hurricane Agnes whipped through Pennsylvania, and the Susquehanna River overflowed its banks. The storm was so swift and sudden that there was no time to prepare. Caskets rose up out of graveyards. Downtown stores were completely destroyed, and thousands of people saw their homes demolished overnight. The area received disaster relief funds from the federal government, with the help of local, influential Democratic Congressman Daniel J. Flood ('29), who enjoyed a thirty-year run in Congress and who had been a customer at our family's grocery store when I was a child.

***

That summer, when so much in Wilkes-Barre was upended and destroyed, including my mother's home, Sy began to experience pain in his back. At first, it wasn't so bad—just a dull, nagging sensation. By the fall, it had turned excruciating. Then, after an x-ray in December, Sy's doctors called and said he needed to come to the hospital immediately for additional tests. Two days later, they summoned us into their office and told us Sy had, at most, ninety days to live. But they didn't know Sy and they didn't know me; from that day forward, I was on a mission to prove his doctors wrong.

***

All this time, during the spring and summer of 1973, the town was growing quickly and anti-Vietnam protests were heating up on the Penn State campus and on campuses across the country. Political controversy overflowed into everyday conversations in State College, and there were noticeable conflicts as well between the professors and townspeople who favored growth and those who were bitterly opposed.

The one and only time I ever said "yes" to filling in for Sy in something other than our business roles was when I was urged by the university to take over the presidency of the State College Chamber of

Commerce. While president of the chamber, I initiated the discussions that led to Penn State taking over management of University Park airport, eventually expanding the runways and bringing the first commercial airplane flights in and out of State College. Prior to that, travelers had to drive more than forty minutes over treacherous windy roads to Black Moshannon airport, where they occasionally had to wait for takeoff or landing until deer cleared off the runway.

As 1973 turned into 1974, we joined the Penn State Alumni Association trip to the Orange Bowl, where we met many new people. Two of them—Della Durant ('57), who was Associate Director of Athletics, and Mac Saddoris (Masters in Counselor Education '75), a graduate student and Methodist minister who gave Sy a copy of *The Prophet* by Kahlil Gibran—became mainstays in our overall support system in what was to be the last year of Sy's life. Sy was in a lot of pain that trip and into the spring. He went through another round of chemotherapy for his back, where the tumors were considerably smaller, but never entirely gone.

Sy was asked to help bring more and better doctors to the Centre Region, and since he was alive, he said "yes." I urged him to preserve his strength, but there was no stopping him. Sy believed he was a walking testament to the miracle of science in treating what were then seen as impossibly aggressive cancers, and whenever he was in remission he did everything he could to help other people.

And then, in the summer of 1974, the cancer got ugly again. Sy's pain was incapacitating much of the time. When he had to be hospitalized again, the doctors told us they believed the cancer had metastasized. That night, we shared the news with our daughters.

In the end, Sy would outlive his doctors' original prognosis by over two years. It was after his death, early in the morning on February 8, 1975, when I found myself as a single mother to two daughters and the sole owner of our business, that my mantra became "Eat first. Cry later."

***

Soon after Sy died, people started approaching me to take his place on various committees and boards on which he had served. I was not sure what I would do next, but I was just forty-one years old.

I knew I needed to do something for myself. I decided not to take on anything "to fill Sy's spot." I wanted to be known and accepted for myself, not as Sy's widow.

Almost immediately, I became attracted to the idea of political office, but the timing was never quite right. Yearning to be thankful—as Sy would have been—for all the life learning we had gathered from those cancer years, the girls and I established the Barash Award for Human Service at Penn State in 1975. And in June, I threw a big party at our house "celebrating gratitude" for Carol's Jewish confirmation and the sheer joy of being alive and available to all the changes going on in every direction.

Three years of bicentennial work came to fruition in the spring of 1976. Back in 1973, through our friend Bob Kunzig in Washington, Barash Advertising won a three-year contract to design, write, and produce print publications for Pennsylvania's celebration of the U.S. bicentennial. That project included a salute to Pennsylvania artists, including Henry Rosenberg, whose painting of Jewish scholars huddling in a dark ghetto was one of many gifts Sy gave me when he first learned of the ninety-day cancer death notice. Though he could barely walk, Sy chartered a private plane to Pittsburgh to visit the artist's studio in Squirrel Hill and pick out the painting.

Also in the spring of 1976 came the first Sy Barash Regatta at Stone Valley Recreation Center with games, canoe races, and an outdoor concert to raise money for the American Cancer Society. And in July, the Arts Festival board decided to honor Sy, too. All of these tributes were bittersweet, filled with memories of the work we'd done together in our early years of marriage and business, but they also pulled me back a bit, when I really wanted to get on with something, though I wasn't sure what.

I had an opportunity to take on women's equality and learn the complexities of many other state and national challenges when I was one of two women elected alumni members of the Penn State Board of Trustees in 1976. One of my first assignments was appointment to the board of the Renaissance Scholarship Fund, which provides scholarships for high-achieving low-income students to Penn State. I had the privilege to serve as the one-person sub-committee tasked with writing the university's response to the Sullivan Principles and our policy to divest from stocks with holdings in South Africa with University Vice President for Finance, Bob Patterson ('62). And I went on the road with Joe Paterno to meet with local alumni chapters in Pennsylvania to get them more involved with the university.

At the exact same time that I was taking on the most important volunteer commitment of my life, we experienced one of our biggest business blunders, a coupon tabloid called "Saving Shopper," an idea I loved which died after just one issue. I saved a copy of that one and only issue, a reminder that everyone fails sometimes, and we often learn the most from our toughest, darkest days.

A year later, in the spring of 1977, our general manager Tom Wheland pointed out State Senator Lou Coppersmith from Johnstown at the Pennsylvanians for Effective Government annual dinner. Lou had recently been widowed, and I walked over to offer my condolences. Not long afterward, Lou called me to take me out to dinner on his way from Johnstown to Harrisburg—not exactly a direct route!

We introduced our children to one another at Thanksgiving and were married the next spring at Eisenhower Chapel on the Penn State campus. Lou helped me make peace with my mother; I made him visit his estranged sister. There was a magic to our relationship, both emotionally and intellectually; he softened some of my rougher edges, and in ten short years of marriage helped me to see what matters most, in my own conduct and in life with my dearest family members.

As my daughters went off to college—Carol to Yale in 1976 and Nan to the University of Arizona in 1979--I was running a successful and growing business and married to the great love of my life, someone who held me to a higher standard than anyone I'd ever known or loved before.

CHAPTER 13
WHAT DO YOU DO FOR AN ENCORE? WORKING WITH JESSE OWENS

One of the most challenging parts of the advertising agency business is the drive to keep generating big, breakthrough creative ideas.

Lesson #12: The great work you do fades quickly. Don't rest on your laurels. Keep thinking about your next big idea.

I think that our steady turnover of talent in the agency was in part because it is such exhausting, high-stakes work. There are no automatic renewals, and few ideas that are sustainable for more than a year or two. The brain-drain in our agency, both my own exhaustion and the revolving door of creative talent, never really went away. Agency work was the creative engine that drove innovation in all parts of our business and was what set us apart from our competitors who did only outdoor advertising, but it was also the least scalable and least sustainable part of our overall business.

Our neighbor and friend, Jim Palmer, was a brilliant and demanding customer, far ahead of his peers in so many ways: developing technology to transmit television signals to the masses, producing amplifiers offshore to save money on labor, and thinking beyond local solutions to the larger infrastructural needs to expand communications nationwide.

Jim used the annual trade show of the National Cable Television Association to showcase his new products and to command industry leadership. By the early 1970s, I was running the advertising for Jim's businesses, and each year, he challenged me to get more and more customers to his booth at the show. Sy and I traveled with Jim to the show, to help him drum up business. In 1970, we offered a meet and greet with Mike Reid ('69), Penn State's All-American defensive lineman, who played piano at the company's booth. For the convention in 1971, we sent a mailing to the top one hundred executives Jim wanted to talk to. The envelope, mailed Special Delivery, included a short letter and the non-negotiable half of a twenty dollar bill. The letter invited company leaders to "Stop at our booth and we'll give you the other half."

Jim told me he'd be very happy if he got to speak with one-third of the people we invited. An amazing fifty-nine recipients stopped by the booth and listened to his pitch. For three who couldn't attend, Jim accepted invitations to present in their offices: a sixty-two percent response rate. We learned later that it was illegal to cut money in half, but I loved the idea so much I never stopped to ask!

***

So, what do you do for an encore? It was 1972, and Jim had just renamed his company C-COR Electronics. It was originally called Community Engineering Corporation, operating as CECO, until they received a cease and desist order from the company that owned that name. To introduce the new name and build on the hype of the Olympics, we recommended that C-COR name their new line of amplifiers "The Olympic Series."

"The best part of the idea," I bravely added when sharing the idea with Jim, having no notion whether I could actually pull it off, "is we'd like to engage Jesse Owens as your company spokesman."

The plan included producing a short video with Jim and Jesse talking about the power of the new amplifier series, filmed at the C-COR plant in State College, and Owens on site in C-COR's booth at the NCTA convention, right before the summer Olympics were about to begin.

Both Barash Advertising and C-COR were young enough to believe we could perform miracles. Jim loved the idea, and so I had to deliver.

I could hear my mother's voice, "The worst they can say is 'no.' If you don't ask, Mimi, you never get."

For one of the most significant negotiations of my lifetime, and certainly the biggest up until then, I simply got lucky. It turned out that Jesse Owens was his own agent, and I was able to track him down on the phone. I called him first in Chicago but learned he had recently moved to Arizona. Eventually, he picked up his own phone, was a delight to talk with, and showed himself to be very relaxed about all the planning. I convinced him to come to State College to narrate a short film about the amplifiers and to go to the convention— for four days—and be at the booth for people to meet him.

Hard to believe, as I look back, that I negotiated with the man who stood up to Adolf Hitler, turning hate into honor at the 1936 Olympics, and whom *Sports Illustrated* named the greatest athlete of all time, to serve as C-COR spokesperson. The convention sponsors introduced Owens at the closing banquet and paid a salute to him. To this day, one of my most rewarding professional moments came from working with Jesse Owens in the spring and summer of 1972.

CHAPTER 14
WHEN OPPORTUNITY KNOCKS, ACCELERATE: CENTRAL COUNTIES BANK

In the early 1970s, the long-time president of First National Bank of State College, John Truby, retired. Charles "Chuck" Grimm, the newly appointed president, invited Sy and me to discuss the proposed merger of First National with Lock Haven Bank & Trust. Orie Claster, our long-time customer, was president of the board of Lock Haven Bank & Trust and recommended that we be considered to provide a fresh direction for the new bank, which brought together two old, deeply established local banks on the cusp of dramatic growth.

For our little advertising agency, this represented not only a very significant piece of business, but one with the possibility of propelling us to a much higher level of regional recognition. It all happened very quickly: we won the assignment to take the new, merged bank to market, starting with nothing but the new name: Central Counties Bank. The assignment included a new logo and branding, as well as a strategic marketing plan for the combined bank.

The new president, Elmer Grant, came from a successful career at Pittsburgh National Bank and urged us to take bold steps in a new direction. He was a tall man, over six feet, kind but demanding, a down-to-earth, clear-speaking community leader. His outlook was refreshing, driving the kind of novelty and innovation that turned me and our team on.

Elmer wanted not only new ideas but fully-developed strategy and planning that most local agencies could not provide. In his first year as president of Central Counties, in rapid succession, Elmer replaced most of the bank's local service providers with larger, national companies. Though Barash Advertising was still very much "College Avenue," not "Madison Avenue," we seized this opportunity to step up our act.

Helping the bank break through the boundaries of Centre County also enabled us to stretch in new directions as an agency.

Most local banks at the time did not have dedicated marketing leadership. Advertising was mostly media placement and usually a small job for someone whose focus was another area of the business: perhaps the person who ran HR or supervised the tellers. But when the two banks merged, Buck Snare from Lock Haven had "Marketing Manager" added to his title, and Elmer, the bank president, closely oversaw the whole process. He attended our Monday morning marketing meetings, and every meeting ended with a list of action items and a deadline for each one. This was a more serious way of doing business than we had ever been previously exposed to, and I loved it.

The centerpiece of our plan was the strategic partnership with Penn State Intercollegiate Athletics at a time when Penn State was emerging onto the national scene in football, men's and women's basketball, gymnastics, and other sports (long before Learfield took over management of Penn State Athletic Properties). Though more costly than other ideas we proposed, the link with Penn State Athletics, and the use of sports as a unifying theme, spoke powerfully to the local community and was designed to draw new customers into the bank in person.

We unequivocally recommended that Central Counties Bank work closely with Penn State Athletics, especially football, which was leading new, national trends in sports marketing. For Central Counties we created everything from wallet-sized printed schedules for each sport to sponsorship of the first electronic scoreboards in Beaver Stadium and Rec Hall. As these new technologies emerged, we made sure Central Counties Bank was the first in line, signing up as the lead sponsor of each one. Though I had never before negotiated six-figure contracts of this nature, I saw it as a great new challenge and never paused to get nervous.

Elmer could be really tough. On one occasion, we presented an overall fall promotion that included a stadium blanket giveaway with new checking accounts. After we showed him the various pieces-- print, point of purchase, radio, TV, and outdoor advertising--Elmer roared, "Go back to the drawing board. I don't like it."

That was like a stab in my heart after all the work involved. I hated that my team had to be subjected to his assault.

71

"Wait a minute Elmer," I suggested, trying to regroup. "Let's review the potential benefits," and I repeated the most salient ones.

He paused for a long time and finally said, "That's what I like about you as a woman, Mimi..." After another seemingly interminable pause, he added, "You've got balls." I honestly think he meant it as a compliment.

Without thinking, feminist me retorted, "I don't know whether to thank you, Elmer, or kick you in yours."

After an extended silence, everyone burst out in laughter, and I noticed I was the only woman in the room. In those days, I was often the only woman in the room but only rarely thought about it.

For me, this was an a-ha moment. His first response could have silenced me, and I could have become timid and submissive.

Lesson #13: When you have established trust in a business relationship, you ought to be able to step up, say what's on your mind and push things forward fearlessly.

***

When Penn State won a spot in the New Year's Day 1972 Cotton Bowl against the Texas Longhorns, I identified an opportunity to introduce a new type of connection between the university and the local business community. I worked up my idea—Penn State booster buttons, sponsored by Central Counties Bank, that said, "Go Penn State, Rattle the Cattle"—and made an appointment to present my idea to Elmer.

I was so excited, I could barely hold in my enthusiasm as I explained the idea to him. For me, it was the first time I presented a "rush idea"—my own concept—at this level.

"What do you think?" I asked him.

"I know a good idea when I see one," Elmer said. "Let's do it. And thanks for bringing it to me first."

To build on the momentum, I called a local billboard company in Dallas and asked if we could use some of their open inventory for billboards with the same message: "Go Penn State, Rattle the Cattle," with our name, Barash Advertising, at the bottom. The owner said yes, so our only cost was screening the posters. From a PR perspective, this was a major coup for our agency. When the billboard was featured on the front page of the *Dallas Times Herald*, friends in Texas sent us copies.

The Booster Buttons had been a huge success for the Cotton Bowl, and I knew we should keep running with them. I brought the idea to Buck Snare, the marketing manager from Lock Haven. People would submit their slogan ideas for each button at the bank. Penn State would review the ideas and pick the winning slogan for each button. And we would supply custom buttons for each home game. Buck loved the idea, but he was a small-town guy and would only commit to one thousand buttons for the first two games.

When the buttons were an instant success—the one thousand gone in the first two days for both games—we really had to scramble to get the slogans picked and the order delivered on time for five thousand buttons for each of the last two home games. Those early buttons, like the early issues of *Town & Gown*, now sell for big bucks on eBay. There was even one rogue button in the 1970s that said, "Shitt on Pitt."

***

Our relationship with Central Counties took us through many mergers: First National Bank of Altoona, First National Bank of Lewistown, Lewisburg, and eventually Mellon Bank and then Citizens Bank. In the early 1980s, the bank brought in a new person to run marketing, and one day, she called my creative team "a bunch of turkeys." I scheduled a meeting with her.

We talked about other things, and then we started to discuss our creative team. I said, "If that's how you really feel about our team, we should think about a plan to phase out."

"When?" she replied.

"How about thirty days?"

That was it. Right there and then, ten years of relationship building and eighteen percent of our agency business out the door in an instant.

The only thing we kept was the Booster Button program for Penn State Football. Those Booster Buttons were by far our blockbuster success with Central Counties Bank, and one that has lasted more than forty-five years, though they almost went down the drain in 2014. By that time, Mellon Bank had merged into Citizens Bank. Learfield had taken over management of Penn State Sports Properties. And PNC had become the exclusive bank sponsor of Penn State Athletics.

For a while, our Booster Buttons for Citizen's Bank stayed below the radar. Then, one cold fall morning, I showed up at the President's tailgate, and there were no Booster Buttons. I knew we had produced the buttons and delivered them to all the Penn State venues where they were usually distributed. When I arrived at the tailgate, I was told that the university staff had received the buttons but were instructed not to distribute them. Though I no longer owned or worked in the business, I was like a mama bear who'd lost her cub. The investigative reporter in me needed to get to the bottom of the situation, and I sent my younger daughter, Nan, who by this point was managing The Barash Group, to figure out how to salvage the deal.

* * *

The buttons live on, but no longer on the Penn State campus. Today, the bank encourages customers to make a contribution of canned goods to their local food bank as part of the Booster Button program. The program extends to bank branches and families in over twenty-five Pennsylvania communities where Penn State has its campuses. In 2016, the three State College branches distributed over 3000 pounds of food and $5502 to the local food bank.

The near loss of the Booster Button program challenged us to make the offer even better for the bank, their customers, and the larger community, which was the whole point of Central Counties' working with Penn State Athletics back in the 1970s.

CHAPTER 15
RIGHT JOB, WRONG TIME: PRESIDENT OF THE CHAMBER OF COMMERCE

In early March 1973, I was engaged in a juggling act trying to manage an overflowing business plate, regular trips to and from Sloan Kettering in New York for Sy's treatments, and struggling to find the confidence to be the kind of mother my daughters needed at the time.

I was walking down Allen Street to get to a meeting at Central Counties Bank one morning when Dave Schuckers ('68), Penn State's government relations representative and President of the State College Chamber of Commerce, stopped me in my tracks. He was on his way to make a cold call on me at my office. Instead, we stood in the blustery cold at the corner of Allen Street and Foster Avenue.

With very little preamble, Dave said to me, "Mimi, you've got to take over the presidency of the chamber."

I thought he'd lost his mind, but I listened.

He told me that a few local business owners were incensed that Penn State was planning to expand the bookstore it owned and operated in the Hetzel Union Building, the main student center on campus. While convenient for students and good for the university, the local business owners perceived this to be in direct competition with the four independent bookstores downtown.

Gary Moyer ('64), a local jeweler, pulled together a small group of disgruntled business owners who testified before the state legislature, representing themselves as the leadership of the local chamber of commerce, which they were not, and stating that they were in opposition to the university's annual appropriation from the Pennsylvania legislature. University President Jack Oswald and his wife, Rose, came back from an extended trip to China, and Jack was livid when he heard the news. In discussions with his top advisors,

Jack proposed that the university, the chamber's largest dues-paying member, drop out of the chamber. To make matters worse, Dave Schuckers, the university's representative to the chamber at that time, was also chamber president.

The message Dave Shuckers delivered to me that day was a compromise: Jack wanted Sy, his trusted friend, to lead the chamber back to its senses and a compromise with the university. But since he knew that wasn't possible while Sy was undergoing chemotherapy, he wanted me to take on the job instead. Dave promised that the university would provide the support I needed to succeed, brokering a desperately needed truce between State College business people and the university on several seemingly intractable issues.

A year later I was named president of the chamber. This was the one and only time I ever took on something intended for, or in place of, my first husband, Sy. When I took this role on, under extremely tense conditions between State College and Penn State, and in my own personal life—only thirty-nine years old, with two daughters, aged fourteen and eleven, and a dying husband—I never imagined how it would catapult me into a leadership role, both in State College and Penn State.

"I never aspired to be a business woman," I often repeat. "I wanted to be an investigative reporter." And, honestly, I still do.

Lesson #14: Think about what makes people tick and why things happen the way they do. Intervene in those stories; listen as best you can to all sides; and lead positive change in your community.

Looking back, my brief experience as emergency president of the chamber enhanced my level of self-confidence and self-esteem and helped me identify my passion to truly make a difference on both sides of College Avenue.

Since it felt like I had little choice in the matter, I decided to make the best of the opportunity that presented itself and move the chamber forward around three vital issues: calming the conflict between Penn State and local business people about the bookstore on campus, which had precipitated my presidency; helping the business community achieve a stronger voice in the local zoning process; and working to get commercial air service from State College to Pittsburgh, Philadelphia, and Washington, D.C.

In order to achieve anything else, the first thing we needed was more open, less confrontational communication between the university and local business people. I encouraged the chamber to take the lead in establishing pathways for better communication on sensitive issues. To this end, we instituted an annual "Town Day" program, in which leaders from the town and the university came together to talk about our mutual challenges in a spirit of collaboration. The tipping point, Penn State's proposed full-service bookstore--including school supplies and Penn State clothing--made it clear that my job was to figure out how we could openly discuss issues like that, where there was an inherent tension and competition between the university and the town. This was the first time I was in the position to lead those discussions, while honoring multiple points of view.

Tensions between the town and the university will probably never go away because the answers to satisfy everyone do not come easily. For these inherently multifaceted issues, negotiating and compromise are the only way to balance conflicting needs and points of view. Trying to rise above the fray and create something that was in the common good, the chamber presidency gave me my first public opportunity to not only figure out and advocate for my sense of what was right, but also to listen to different sides and help facilitate the best answer for all parties involved.

As president of the chamber, many of the issues I was involved in transformed the community in ways that are still unfolding. Perhaps the biggest change was the university's decision—in a bow to local business people—to stop building more dorms. This shift significantly benefited local developers, who made a fortune in the student apartment rental business in the later 1970s and since.

***

All of these issues—the bookstore, housing, zoning, and the airport—resulted from the extraordinarily rapid growth of the student population during this period. This growth has now leveled off, but the challenges remain. All over town, we have neighborhoods with houses designed for single families being converted to student housing, dramatically undermining the peaceful quality of those neighborhoods. This problem is most pronounced on football weekends, when many local people rent out their houses as party venues for a few thousand dollars a weekend.

Homan Avenue, where Sy and I raised our children, is a good example. Once a beautiful sleepy street on the southern edge of town, now some of the homes on the block just off Pugh Street have been purchased by real estate speculators and turned into student housing. There is trash in the front yards, noise late at night, and overall deterioration of the homes. That's what begins to happen when housing density increases and students pack into what were originally designed as single-family homes.

Renting to students is often more lucrative than selling to single families, driving realtors to make tough decisions about their own and the community's welfare. When local neighborhoods begin to collapse, homeowners form neighborhood associations to keep students out, and tensions keep escalating. These are problems that touch every college town.

Looking from the vantage point of the present, local business owners were right to be wary in the 1970s. As a long-term result of the Barnes & Noble bookstore on campus, there is now only one full-fledged, privately owned bookstore downtown, the Student Bookstore. But now, in another turn, both local merchants and small retail businesses on campus face similar challenges from internet shopping, which has now appeared in the flesh in downtown State College, with Amazon leasing space for a distribution center smack dab in the middle of Allen Street, on the site of what was once McLanahan's, one of the three original soda fountains in town.

The university and the business community now collaborate on projects that we could not have imagined in the 1970s. Today, the university leads an ambitious, cooperative program to produce measurable economic development in the area, turning students' innovative ideas into businesses that provide jobs and sustain the local community. New programs include Penn State's working partnership with the Chamber of Business and Industry (CBICC) through programs like Invent Penn State, the Launch Box, and many smaller incubator projects. Through a shared infrastructure, student innovators receive free banking, legal, and marketing advice.

Over the last twenty years, substantial local businesses have evolved from this cooperative effort, including Videon Central,

Minitab, and Restek. The goal of all these programs is to foster students' great ideas, like Schreyer Honors College graduate Mary Elizabeth McCulloch ('16) and her Project Vive device, which gives voice to people who can't speak, and to help take more of them successfully to market.

Innovation and entrepreneurship often flourish in college towns. The conflicts of the 1970s and the new ways of communicating that emerged as a result have driven a spirit of collaboration that exists to this day. For me, the chamber presidency was a major catalyst to becoming a visible community leader building viable solutions to tough, ongoing but also solvable problems that look different from different points of view.

CHAPTER 16
COMMANDER MODE: SY BATTLES CANCER

When the Susquehanna River overflowed its banks during Hurricane Agnes, my mother's ground floor apartment in Wilkes-Barre was flooded. My mother called us, hysterical, from my cousin Sarah's house in "The Heights," the less affluent side of Wilkes-Barre, but away from the storm's most devastating damage. When the roads opened up again, a week later, we drove to Wilkes-Barre to help my mother clean up and plan her move into temporary housing. All of her keepsakes, even prized family photos hanging above the couch, were destroyed in the water and sludge. Only one set of green glass dishes with gold trim survived in the highest kitchen cabinet. We packed them up in newspaper and brought them home to State College in the trunk of our car.

When Sy reached into the trunk to take out one of the boxes, I could see the grimace on his face. He doubled over in pain, and our neighbors' son carried the boxes into our basement. Sy spent most of that summer in bed, knocked out by the painkillers local doctors prescribed for his back pain.

That fall, my mother moved to an apartment in Parkway Plaza, a complex built by the Woscob family near the State College High School. Through connections at the Convention and Visitors Bureau, we were able to rent a private plane to fly to my nephew's bar mitzvah in Massachusetts in October. Bent over and grimacing, Sy was in so much pain by the time we landed he had to be carried out of the plane.

For the rest of 1972, Sy was in excruciating pain even with the medication and exercises prescribed by the local orthopedists. I finally ran out of patience in early December and insisted that the doctors take x-rays of his back. I made that call from the phone on the kitchen wall, while the kids were eating their breakfast. And then, starting a habit of suspending the rules in times of crisis, I drove them to school, so they wouldn't have to take the bus.

Two days later, when the doctor called us into the office and told us Sy had three months to live, we asked what our plan should be.

"Do whatever you want. Go to the Sugar Bowl like you planned. There's nothing we can do."

I went into commander mode immediately, staying hunkered down for the next two decades of my life. That night, the first night of Hanukkah, December 8, 1972, we told our daughters, "Daddy has cancer," sparing them the ninety-day death sentence the local doctors had given us.

We relented and let our kids get a "Hanukkah Bush" that year and the next two, in imitation of their Christian friends. I bought them extravagant presents and did my best to hold everything together, but looking back, I was not home nearly enough during those rocky, cancer-driven years.

We called our key employees into our living room on Saturday morning and made a plan to get through the coming days and weeks. I smoked incessantly at that time, and I kept copious notes on yellow legal pads, handing over day-to-day responsibilities to employees we felt could manage more to help us through the months and battles ahead.

Monday morning, the first person I went to see was Gene Lee, president of People's National Bank, who held our business loans and checking account. I shut the door and began crying.

I said, "I need to know, Gene, if this goes down the way it might, that you won't put us out of business."

"Mimi, your credit is good with us. Let me know how I can help."

For the first time in my life, I learned to let my guard down and ask the questions that were really on my mind. It's hard to underestimate how much my thinking and decision-making in those days were driven by my fear of failure and loss.

Lesson #15: Women—working to be perfect, and afraid to admit weakness—sometimes have a hard time learning to admit that help is needed.

I had a very hard time making this shift and learning to ask others to help me. But there was so much swirling around me, I had to ask for help in case I needed it later. For as hard as things were, I knew much tougher times lay ahead.

Sy scheduled an appointment that week with local photographer Peter Bruce and had his picture taken before starting any of his cancer treatments.

In addition to running the business, I was also on a marathon to beat the clock on Sy's cancer. We quickly identified Memorial Sloan Kettering Cancer Center in New York as the most advanced cancer hospital in the country, and I made it my job to get Sy in to see the experts there to find out what might be done. Several times a day, I called the person who managed their admissions schedule and worked our way up the waiting list, working every contact I had.

On January 21, 1973, the admissions manager from Sloan Kettering told me they had an opening the next day. Our friends and clients, Barb and Jay Claster, had us flown from University Park airport to Teterboro in New Jersey in their plane with their pilot, Ron Cotner ('63). The Clasters made us reservations at their favorite Hotel Elysée and paid for everything: our lodging, food, and even bringing friends with me to get through the early painful trips to New York and Sloan Kettering. This was something they would do many, many times over the next two years, enabling Sy to receive the best medical treatment available, which we could not have afforded without their help.

Led by Dr. Robert Golby, the Sloan Kettering team identified the primary cancer as adenocarcinoma of the left lung with extensive bone metastases to the back, which were causing Sy's back pain. They operated on Sy, implanting radioactive seeds instead of removing his lung. As soon as he recovered from surgery, they began treating his back with radiation and lots of chemotherapy.

Sy lost the rest of his hair, but he was given a miracle: by the time we reached the end of that original ninety-day sentence, he was on his way back to health, and besides the side effects of chemotherapy (there were few medicines to manage those side effects in the early 1970s), we had a somewhat normal life from April 1973 to August 1974, outside of monthly trips back and forth to see the doctors at Sloan Kettering.

When Sy traveled to New York, I went with him, packing up all the paperwork for billing and client projects and bringing it with me, so I could keep the business running. On the outside, I think it looked like everything was fine, but inside, I was almost eaten alive by the fear and confusion of being out of control.

Barbara Claster, a dear friend and clinical psychologist, offered again and again to get me help, but I always said, "I don't need help. I can get through this. You don't need to worry about me."

I needed answers and read everything I could find about Sy's specific cancer. It seemed likely to me that the seeds of Sy's cancer were planted when he was in the second Marine division that landed at Nagasaki to do cleanup after the U.S. dropped the second atomic bomb there. I reached out to other women whose husbands had been at Hiroshima and Nagasaki during the war, and many were struggling with similar small cell cancers and leukemias. I wrote to our Congressman and Senators, but no one took this connection seriously at the time.

On the home front, a string of families stayed with Carol and Nan whenever Sy and I traveled to New York for treatment. This was not an ideal solution, but it was the best I could pull together at the time.

As soon as Sy was back on his feet, he very much wanted to thank the people who had enabled us to get started in business. Being publicly philanthropic for the first time, we established the General W. A. Morgan Award at the Altoona Campus of Penn State to honor a male and female ROTC student for their scholarship, leadership, and service each year.

When Sy gave out the awards the first year, he said, "Though we paid him for his time, there is not enough we can ever repay General Morgan for all that he did to help us on our way in business."

***

But things took a turn for the worse in the summer of 1974. Sy's back pain increased; he was dizzy, confused, and not interested in going to the office. On the day before Nixon resigned, August 8, 1974, I watched the news in Louise Jr restaurant in New York with my cousin, Fred Grossman, while taking a break from Sy's tests at Sloan Kettering.

The doctors said, "If it's what we think it is, bone and brain metastases, he has at most six months to live."

I called the girls, telling them for the first time that it really didn't look like their father was going to get better. There were no cell phones yet, and after that call, perhaps the hardest of my life, I left my wallet in the phone booth at Sloan Kettering. On top of everything else, I had to replace all of my IDs and credit cards.

Sy came home a couple weeks later, but he was never really himself again. He was given another round of aggressive chemotherapy—this last one with an experimental number, not a name. The treatment left him listless and depressed, and even the most basic tasks, such as getting dressed, eating, and talking, exhausted him. There was one night when Carol and Nan invited a few friends over to play Scrabble with Sy, and he left the room in tears, unable to remember even basic words.

That night, I took him to the emergency room at Centre Community Hospital. I stayed up all night with him, a stenographer taking notes while he moaned into the night. The next day the local doctors called Sloan Kettering and followed their instructions to treat the psychosis unleashed as a side effect of chemotherapy. Between chemotherapy and steroids, Sy had a brief reprieve, but in December we were back in Sloan Kettering with few options. We were offered the choice of an unnamed and unproven chemotherapy, which Sy decided not to try.

"I want to go home," he said. "Please take me home."

The black and white pictures from that last Hanukkah at home are hard to look at: Sy's face is puffy and misshapen. His pajamas have food stains, and he really cannot smile. I could feel his pain, but could do nothing to lessen it. We had done everything together, and I was starved not only for his love, but also for his advice, his companionship, and his common sense in business.

In truth, I was almost never home that last fall of Sy's illness. I slept on the living room couch with papers strewn all over the floor. I left the house early in the morning, sometimes before the girls were even awake. I was struggling to keep the business functioning, to pay our employees on time, and to take care of everything at home as best I could.

When Sy returned home for the last time in mid-January, we hired nurses to take care of him during the day. I organized a huge party at our house for our twenty-first wedding anniversary, January 31, 1975. My friends helped with the cooking: a lavish spread that covered the entire kitchen table: shrimp, cold cuts, fresh vegetables and dip, deviled eggs, and much more. And since I never baked, I asked all of our friends to bring desserts! Sy put on clean pajamas and propped himself up in bed, and our friends went back to see him, one by one.

***

When Sy died eight days later, at 5:52 a.m, I was at the office, gathering up my papers for a Pennsylvania Cable Television Association meeting in Pittsburgh that afternoon. Nan heard Sy fall on the floor, and the girls kicked into action.

Carol called me, speaking very fast, "Daddy fell out of bed, and we can't wake him." Before she called me she had called our across-the-street neighbors, Jim and Barb Palmer, and then the ambulance.

I rushed home, and when I got there, Barb was giving him CPR. The paramedics arrived soon after I did and carried his body out.

The next week is largely a blur. I sent Jay Claster and Jim Palmer to select cemetery plots for me and Sy in the Jewish section of Centre County Memorial Park, which our contribution had helped to make possible years before. I called Sy's friend, Mac Saddoris, to give the eulogy.

Lesson #16: Sometimes in life you just keep going.

The girls and I sat *shiva* for the next week, and we continued to go to synagogue to say memorial prayers for thirty days, rituals that connected us to Jewish tradition in a way that had largely lapsed from our assimilated home. It was a very rough time, and I was in so much pain myself I was not really able to help the girls get through. Though we never talked about it, Nan, who was thirteen, and I became very close during that mourning period.

Carol asked for types of help that went against my belief that we would--and should--get through this horrible loss together. Carol's moods were large and frightening her last year at home before she went away to college. Carol remembers pleading with me to help her find a therapist. Though I can't remember that discussion, therapy was something I couldn't begin to imagine at the time. I leaned on Nan, and compared Nan and Carol, in ways that were corrosive and damaging to both of them. I am not surprised that Carol felt left out at the time. This is one of those very painful things I would do differently if I had the chance.

CHAPTER 17
HONORING SY BARASH: THE BARASH AWARD FOR HUMAN
SERVICE AND THE SY BARASH REGATTA

When Sy was diagnosed with terminal lung cancer in December, 1972, his soul came to life at an even faster pace than when he had begun our swift romance.

Sy became quite impulsive and completely unstoppable about his biggest ideas. He put all of his energy into responding to the needs of others; this was true before he had cancer, and even more so in his last two precious years.

We both realized that local doctors had missed diagnosing his cancer for a full year and that he had weird symptoms that should have given pause much sooner: first there was purpura, then hepatitis, plus intermittent periods of exhaustion and a cough that came and went for more than a year, though he was never a smoker. I was furious and sought someone or something to blame.

But Sy had a different approach, urging me to join him as volunteer co-chair of the local Cancer Crusade, an old-school, door-to-door fundraising effort led by the American Cancer Society. In 1974, we raised over $42,000, a twenty-five percent increase over the previous year. Even that failed to meet Sy's need to give back. Spring Week at Penn State had faded into oblivion, and Sy felt the university needed some sort of spring event to get students involved in community service.

Sy urged his fraternity, Beta Sigma Rho, along with Kappa Delta sorority, to sponsor the event and launched with a Mike Reid concert in Schwab Auditorium in 1974.

***

After Sy's death I wanted to honor his unwavering spirit of service. I talked to the girls, and we decided to establish an annual award recognizing a member of the Penn State community who embodied this spirit. In the beginning, someone from town who knew Sy served on the selection committee each year. Today, with the passing of time, there are fewer people alive who actually knew him. The array of recipients of this award would please Sy very much, and I truly enjoy knowing and honoring the diverse individuals who have won the Barash Award.

The very first recipient in 1975 was Bob Welch ('75), who is often credited with bringing the Penn State mascot, the now-famous Nittany Lion, to life on the football field. A former wrestler, he created and set the bar for those now-famous one-arm post-touchdown push-ups.

Quite by accident, getting to know Bob created a remarkable experience for our still-modest advertising agency. Welch's family owned Boyt, a company that manufactured high-end luggage. Bob, a gregarious young man bubbling with ideas, wanted to convince designer Diane Von Furstenberg to transform their private line into Diane Von Furstenberg signature luggage. Our team wrote the script and produced the film for his pitch, our first such endeavor. Diane Von Furstenberg loved the idea, and went on to strike a luggage deal with another supplier!

This project showed us that even without Sy, the Barash team could do something completely new when we all pulled together. I became increasingly ambitious to try new things; I felt that was what Sy would have wanted me to do. Similarly, the Penn State students Sy had touched in his waning months wanted to complete the project he'd started with them: the big, outdoor event based in volunteerism and giving back to the community.

The idea started with four guys from Sy's fraternity, including Brett Eisman ('74) and Andy Bergstein ('74), sitting in front of the fireplace in our living room on Homan Avenue in the spring of 1974. I sat in a chair, off to the side, while they were in a heated discussion about how to pull it off. Sy was so sick, but it was like he was a college student all over again when he was talking to those young men from his fraternity. His last negotiation, just weeks before he died, was convincing the university to allow the fraternity to use Stone Valley Recreation Area for the first Regatta in 1975.

That first year after Sy's death, seeing thousands of students and community members outside, listening to music and engaged in sports and games together, I felt as if Sy was watching and smiling on the whole thing. In the pictures, my two daughters are wearing Regatta t-shirts in different colors and boat-racing together.

Through the 1980s and '90s, the Regatta organizers had to work through fears and realities around binge drinking and increased drug consumption on and off campus. There was no way to limit alcohol consumption at the event, and students often started drinking before they left campus. In 1982, a drunk student was seriously injured diving into a shallow part of the lake, dampening the whole event. Yet crowds increased each year. In 1983, the Regatta was moved from Stone Valley to Bald Eagle State Park in Howard, a bit farther away but still in Centre County. First the university and then the state increased the fees they charged to the fraternity to cover insurance and to dissuade the student organizers from continuing the event.

Each year we'd kickoff the planning with a meeting at the fraternity. I enlisted the president of the university, or the next highest executive who was available, to help these young people know what an important thing they were doing: they were giving of themselves to the challenge of finding a cure for all forms of cancer. We wanted them to feel that their work on the Regatta was part of the solution.

How they responded to this rallying cry was the measure of how well these young men would do at the actual work each year. The occasions that they sat quietly were low years. And the years they excelled could be sensed right at the start—in how they sat, their body language, and the questions they asked. After a year of dismal weather and a big financial loss in 1992, Rich Bundy ('93) and Jeff Jubelirer ('93) moved the event to the fields across from Beaver Stadium in 1993 and ended the Sy Barash Regatta tradition with one of the most successful events ever.

Over nearly twenty years of Regattas, my greatest memory is of my feet sinking into the sand at Stone Valley and the feeling of what young people can do with the right direction and spirit. This was part of my overall healing from the loss of Sy. When those young people worked together, when they triumphed, he was there in all his glory. When I was cleaning out my house to move in 2008, I took my huge collection of Regatta t-shirts and had a local quilter make a quilt for each of Sy's two grandsons, both of whom are named after him.

CHAPTER 18
SO YOU WANT TO BE A STATE SENATOR OR A CONGRESSWOMAN? MOVING ON

In my moments of fantasy, as a young woman, I imagined I might thrive as an elected official. I think the idea was ignited at the Jewish Community Center in Wilkes-Barre, when I was elected vice president of the middle school social club, and the idea was fanned each time I was given the opportunity to speak and lead others publicly.

I received a Senatorial Scholarship to Penn State from State Senator Patrick Toole, who was a customer in our family's grocery store. I remember he sometimes came into our store smelling like alcohol. In many ways, local politics were not much different than today: mostly white men, many of them religious, and not the best educated. Daniel Flood, our Congressman, was a customer in our store too. Completely unforgettable, he was a big guy with a waxed, handlebar mustache. I was a kid, and he acted like I was important. Plus, he took the time to be nice to my mother when he was in the store.

My first effort to put the dream of public office to the test was a race for State College Borough Council in the 1960s. I bought a special outfit at Simmonds in Altoona for my publicity photo. It was a two-piece knit suit in various shades of green. I printed up little brochures that said "This I Believe," long before NPR was even started in 1970. My daughter Carol remembers going door-to-door with me on Nimitz Avenue and handing out those little brochures.

I ran because I wanted to be a part of the decision-making for our community. I thought my ideas were worthwhile. I wanted to help make solutions that served everyone. I loved getting out and talking to people about local issues like zoning, water conservation, and preserving farms in places where development would damage the water supply. I remember feeling very proud and confident.

The only woman in the mix, I came in fifth out of six candidates.

Lesson #17: It takes more than a dream or even a platform to get elected.

And I realized—for the first time really—that I was a rare combination in this part of the world: a progressive, a business owner, and a woman.

And then I moved on to make my mark through business and other types of community service.

In late 1975, when I was beginning to get my bearings again after Sy's death, State Senator Robert "Bobby" Jubelirer ('59) of Altoona and Minority Republican Leader Henry "Merc" Hager ('63) of Williamsport made an appointment to see me in my office. They announced that they'd identified me to run for the State Senate seat that had been held by Joe Ammerman ('50) of Clearfield, who had recently been elected to Congress. This was the same Joe Ammerman who'd helped us fend off Pittsburgh Outdoor when he was a U.S. attorney. The empty seat would be filled in a special election in May 1976.

My spontaneous response: "You must be kidding."

They went on to explain that they had completed a survey, and I had placed second—behind Joe Paterno—in terms of overall local name recognition and viability as a candidate. My views were wide-ranging, so I would appeal to voters from both parties. In that moment, I was shocked, but also intrigued by the idea.

Talking half to myself and half to them, I said, "But I'm in no position to do it. I'm working at keeping this business together and growing it while I also must do a better job as a single parent of two daughters."

They promised to provide an acting CEO to manage my business through the campaign.

What they and I didn't know was that a young male Centre County commissioner, J. Doyle Corman, would challenge me without the party's endorsement. At the nominating convention in the Centre County courthouse, I handily won Centre County, but Doyle snagged all the Clearfield County votes and won 18-15. Ordinarily, it's very hard for me to accept defeat. But in this case, defeat sent an almost soothing message: "It's not the right time for this; I've got enough on my plate right now."

Two years later, when Ammerman's first term peeked over the horizon, Jubelirer, Hager and Cliff Jones ('73), Executive of Pennsylvanians for Effective Government, a Republican businessmen's lobbying group, came to me to run for Congress to unseat Ammerman at the end of his first term, when he was most vulnerable. I had serious doubts, but I agreed to think about it and reconvene to discuss it further. Unbeknownst to them, although I was still a registered Republican (who hardly ever voted that way), I had begun to date State Senator W. Louis Coppersmith in May 1976, so I sought his advice.

Lou said, "I'll be glad to contribute to your campaign. I'd like to see you beat him. He's not my kind of colleague--not dependable."

At that moment, I would have preferred Lou to discourage me from running. In my heart, I truly hoped something would come of this relationship. But Lou was too much of a feminist to stop me from pursuing my dream.

I remember vividly when Bill Clinger, who was also considering running against Ammerman, came to my home in December 1977 to talk about our competing candidacies. I shared with him that I wasn't sure I wanted to run, even though there was pressure on me to do so. We agreed that only one of us should enter the election.

He went on to win that race, and he served in Congress for eighteen years. He was one of thirty former Republican elected officials to publicly oppose the candidacy of Donald Trump. In his memoir, Clinger said that my stepping aside had made it possible for him to win his first run for Congress.

That first race, I put my energy behind Clinger, a practicing attorney from an affluent family in Warren, Pennsylvania, who had attended Johns Hopkins and the University of Virginia Law School. Clinger struck me as a balanced and thoughtful leader. I had just been elected to the Penn State Board of Trustees, and I felt that was a much better fit for my talents. I just couldn't convince myself to make such a complete change in professional direction.

It was one of the very few times I've not taken on this type of public opportunity.

CHAPTER 19

TARGETING MY SPECIFIC PUBLIC SERVICE: A NEW TYPE
OF TRUSTEE

I never really contemplated or prepared for widowhood. We concentrated with all our being on the hope that Sy would recover. Looking back, on another level, I had been preparing myself emotionally the entire time, and even while grieving, I jumped into the rest of my life with both feet.

I was only forty-one, and I had to decide who I wanted to be: would I remain Mrs. Sy Barash (like the name over my office door; "Mrs. B" for short) or create my own new identity as Mimi Ungar Barash? I started to ask myself the question Sy often asked, "What makes Mimi run?"

My first test came when I was asked to replace Sy on the Farmer's National Bank board. Though I would have been the first woman on their board, I declined—first, because no one could really replace Sy, and second, because I needed to determine what would best suit my interest and capability. Finance was not my forte, and we had several other bank clients.

Because Penn State was so central to my own life and such a force for good in our community, I decided that I should seek one of the alumni seats on the board of trustees. No question that it was a long shot, but that made me want it even more. I felt that I was a different type of candidate, someone who grew up poor, who was not an education, politics, or business insider, and who had lived and worked my entire life at the intersection of town and gown.

I sought the advice of the most powerful players I knew at the university: Roy Wilkinson ('36), Counsel to Penn State, later a Pennsylvania Supreme Court Justice; Ridge Riley ('32) and Ross Lehman ('42), Alumni Association executives; and W. K. "Bill"

Ulerich ('31), chair of the Penn State board and owner of media outlets with whom we did a lot of business. None were overly optimistic about my chances. Bill offered to help. Roy was very helpful but felt, as a Jewish woman, I'd lose the first time and should use this effort to lay the groundwork to win the next time. Ridge and Ross sounded lukewarm, at best, but it was very difficult to read exactly what they really felt. Their ambivalence might have had something to do with the fact that the Alumni Association pretty much controlled the alumni trustee selection process, and they didn't like the idea of candidates who put themselves forward. After those meetings, though I knew it would be a tough process and not a sure thing, I decided to give it my best shot.

At the time, my critics said that I politicized the alumni trustee election process, but I had a goal. I was running to win. I recruited a committee of one hundred people to endorse my candidacy openly and enlisted as many of those as possible to actively participate in communicating directly with their Penn State circle of friends. I prepared a four-color brochure with the committee members' names on the back, provided sample letters for them to select from and use in mailing ten to twenty-five letters each that also asked the recipients to do the same. I wrote to a cross-section of alumni clubs, and to those within a few hours' drive from State College, I offered to come and speak at a club meeting. I traveled to Allentown, Philadelphia, Altoona, and Pittsburgh, but concentrated heavily on the greater State College area where the highest number of alumni lived.

When I heard that Barbara Hackman Franklin ('62) had entered the race, I wanted to cry. Barbara was extremely qualified in ways that many people respected. She was in the first class of fourteen women to get an MBA from Harvard in 1964, and she brought both corporate leadership from her work at Singer and First National City Bank (laying the foundation for what became Citibank) and a continuous record of government service as the woman responsible for getting more women appointed to the Nixon administration. She scared me more than a little. How could I, a liberal, Jewish, first-generation college graduate, widow, and self-made business woman possibly beat a white Anglo-Saxon Protestant Republican and political insider?

Up to that point, there had been only one woman elected in the history of Penn State alumni trustee elections: Helen Wise in 1969. I assumed it was impossible for both Barbara Franklin and me to win. So what did I do? I picked up the phone, called Barbara, and asked her not to run. I tried to make the case that two women couldn't win against three seasoned, white male incumbents. I shared my prediction that she would take first place because of her experience in national government.

Barbara said, "Mimi, I think we can both win. We're not running *against* one another."

That call made me even more determined to win. But it did change my approach, and I ran on my own merits, not against Barbara. In the end, we were both right. Barbara did come in first; second was incumbent Michael Baker ('59); and I came in third, with just a few more votes than the incumbent George Deike ('31), who came in fourth.

To say I was ecstatic would be an understatement. Transformational in so many ways, this victory became the beginning of the rest of my life. As a Penn State trustee, I watched and learned from people with so much more experience, savvy, and all-around capabilities than I had at the time.

My first Trustee meeting in July 1977 was at the Behrend Campus. My debate experience taught me to ask good questions while I got my footing. Though I was identified—and identified myself—as an outsider, I slowly learned how to be an effective insider, while finding ways to be a strong advocate for the underserved at Penn State and the larger world.

My first two official assignments on the board were relatively minor. I was appointed to the Renaissance Scholarship board and the Affirmative Action Committee, both of which struggled for status and priority at the time. I took these assignments seriously and used them as opportunities to learn and build allies on the board.

Barbara was right about this too: I didn't need to think of myself as a party of one anymore. Working together with the other women trustees—including Helen Wise ('49 '52MEd, '68Ded), Barbara Franklin, Cecile Springer, a gubernatorial appointee, and Caryl Kline, the Pennsylvania Secretary of Education—we pushed for a study on the Status of Women at Penn State to help determine an agenda for future action. Many improvements flowed from that initial study of the inequities faced by women at the university.

In 1986, we established the Administrative Fellows Program to prepare more women for administrative leadership, and in 1989, the program was extended to include men from underrepresented groups. We also launched the major in Women's Studies and funded the Julia Gregg Brill ('21) Professorship in Women's Studies, honoring Penn State's first woman faculty member.

Lesson #18: Good leaders demonstrate courage in their convictions. They get things done, and they move on.

CHAPTER 20
BRINGING ENTREPRENEURIAL SPIRIT TO PUBLIC SERVICE: THE BIRTH OF THE RENAISSANCE FUND

In 1969, Helen Wise, Jesse Arnelle ('55, '62 Law), and Gilbert "Ott" Nurick ('28, '31 Law) sought election as a renegade slate of alumni to the Penn State Board of Trustees. Their platform included unseating alumni-elected incumbents who acted as a rubber-stamp on university administration, reorganizing the board structure to have more open governance, and running future meetings with increased transparency.

A group of outspoken alumni, spearheaded by Phoebe Forrest Link ('49), an alumna who lived in town and whose husband worked at the university, drove a very public selection process that ultimately elected Wise and Arnelle, unseated longstanding trustees John L. "Blondie" Romig ('21) and B. C. Jones ('16). The university agreed to increase the number of full board meetings from two to seven per year (this was later reduced to six). And, most importantly, they replaced a system in which an eight-member Executive Committee, chaired by cigar-smoking Cappy Rowland ('17) for seven years, met behind closed doors to make the most important decisions.

Going against the usual way of doing business and shocking some long-standing board members and administrators, Jesse and Helen enlisted several sitting members of the board to join this movement for fair and open university governance: Michael Baker, Ralph Dorn Hetzel ('33), Charles Dowd, and Fritz Close ('28). Over a relatively short period of time, the university agreed to support substantive change to the board's operations. This included a full working committee structure and opening all committee meetings to all trustees, so there was far less secrecy.

The need for a more diverse student body hung like a dark cloud over these discussions about how to make Penn State governance more fair and democratic. Though seventy-eight percent of the Pennsylvania population lived in urban areas, the university focused very little attention on the needs of inner-city students and the hurdles they faced gaining admission to the university. The need for more scholarships became a rallying cry for more change.

The Renaissance Fund, approved at the first full board meeting after Helen and Jesse were elected as alumni trustees in 1969, was the university's answer to this crisis. They contributed (and still do) $40,000 per year to an endowed scholarship fund for "the best of the neediest of a diverse student body." The Renaissance Fund was a lightning rod for change, attracting many local alumni to contribute to the university for the first time. Former professional football player Rosey Grier ('56) helped to raise money from far-flung alumni, and "Ott" Nurick contributed all the legal work to establish the fund at no cost to the university. A large and diverse board, including students, faculty, alumni, trustees, and townspeople, was established to oversee the Fund's progress.

My first significant work as a trustee was as a member of the Renaissance Fund board, led at the time by Arthur "Duke" Wellington, director of Counselor Education. The Renaissance Fund was really a perfect assignment for me: it was a big idea, with unlimited potential to help students like myself for whom a Penn State education could make a lasting difference in their own and their family's destiny.

I raised my hand at my first Renaissance board meeting and asked, "What are we doing to grow contributions? $40,000 is not a lot of money. What can we do to help more students?"

I may have asked my questions one at a time; more likely they came out quickly, as an idea formed in my mind.

"How about an annual dinner to honor a living leader who exemplifies what the university stands for, someone who is recognized for service in both the town and the university."

We held the first planning meeting on campus in the Keller Building, after the November 1976 trustee meeting. As the only member of the first dinner committee who was active both in town and on campus, I was asked to recommend the honoree.

I arrived knowing who I thought the honoree should be: Jo Hays

('23), who had a career as superintendent of the local schools, had served as a state senator, and was about to retire as mayor of State College. The committee agreed. Jo had been a strong voice for the university in local and state government and was also someone who helped to articulate the community's point of view to the university.

I continued making the final decision independently until the fourth dinner when Jerome Weinstein ('38), editor of the *Centre Daily Times*, asked me how the selection was made. A tad embarrassed, I responded, "I decide." He advised me to seek broader input from the community and to expand the dinner committee beyond the official Renaissance Fund board. This was great advice, which changed the future of the decision. Now we have a rolling list of prospective honorees for recognition, and each year we seek additional candidates for consideration.

The first dinner raised $8600 in scholarships funds; more recently, we raise several hundred thousand at the annual dinner each year. And at the end of fiscal year 2017, the Renaissance Fund endowment stands at more than $12.6 million, enabling hundreds of low-income and first-generation students to attend Penn State, who would not have had the means without the university's support. We are also working to spread the dinners to all commonwealth campuses to increase the number of Renaissance Scholarships available in their local communities.

Held on the second or third Wednesday or Thursday of November, preferably before a home football game, the dinner has become a major annual community event supported by people from all walks of life. The presence of Renaissance Scholarship recipients at each table and a student speaker provide evidence of the impact of these need-based scholarships. Ironically, the most successful dinner we never had, in terms of funds raised (over $700,000) was to honor Sandy and Graham Spanier. But that dinner was cancelled following the indictment of Jerry Sandusky on multiple counts of sexual abuse of young boys.

CHAPTER 21
THINGS I LEARNED TO TALK ABOUT: SINGLE IN MY 40S

Sexual harassment, rape, emotional and physical abuse pervade the lives of many women—as many as forty percent by some estimates—and hold many of us back. Yet it is something many are afraid to talk about openly. I think one of the ways I survived over the years was to block out things that were so unpleasant I didn't want to talk about them, or even think about them, in some cases. I was too afraid and embarrassed to admit some of the things I was exposed to because I am a woman.

The first incident I can remember I was about fourteen. I was walking from my home in Kingston over the bridge to Wilkes-Barre to an activity at the JCC. I went there after school often. Out of the corner of my eye, I saw a middle-aged man, at the top of the steps leading down to the banks of the Susquehanna River, dangling his penis out of his pants and starting to move toward me. I shifted into high gear and ran the rest of the way to the JCC on South River Street. I called the police as soon as I got there, but they didn't take me seriously. Though they said they'd check it out and get back to my family, it actually felt like they were dismissing my account entirely. You can bet I never walked alone over that bridge again. But looking back, I see how that event left me bewildered and confused in ways I was never able to put into words.

As a young married woman, during my first dentist appointment in State College, the dentist brushed his hand over my right breast during the exam. I sat up and proclaimed, loud enough for his staff to hear, "Don't you dare do that again!" And he never did.

The next time, a few years later, still lingers as unbelievable, and excruciatingly embarrassing, to me. When the husband of a friend and neighbor came knocking on our door to see our newborn daughter, Carol, in October, 1958, I was naive enough to believe he had good intentions. Once I put Carol back in her crib, he fondled my breasts and attempted to do more. Happily, my strength out-performed his, and I chased him out the door.

"Get out and never come back," I ordered. Hard to believe, but I couldn't find the courage to tell his wife. And I never told my husband either.

Worst of them all was a blind date with a bank president from a neighboring county. Our general manager thought he'd be a nice date for me as I began to adjust to being a single woman, widow, and mom in 1976, at age forty-two. I trusted my employee's judgement, so I said the banker could give me a call at home about possibly escorting me to a local fundraising event. He sounded like a gentleman by phone: good sense of humor, interested in theater, and a graduate of the University of Pennsylvania. I had no idea he was married, and no one bothered to tell me.

I felt the time had arrived for me to start "dating" again, so I agreed to have him pick me up and drive me to the event. Of course, all eyes were on us: two reasonably prominent folks together for the first time. I must confess, I had a wonderful time at the party. He was a great dancer, one of the few skills my devoted and loving husband Sy never acquired.

When it was time to return home to Nan (Carol was off at Yale by this point), he insisted on coming in to chat. He sat down in the living room, and when I came back from the kitchen with a glass of water, the next thing I know he jumped up from his seat, pushed me down on the couch and tried to unzip my cocktail dress.

Somehow, I managed to force him away and push him out the door. I never saw him again.

Finally, one that blew me away involved a Penn State administrator who was a prominent member of our synagogue. He couldn't have been more helpful to me, taking care of myriad details that are nearly impossible after you've suffered a serious loss. He ran to the courthouse for me, delivered important papers to the office on days I worked from home, shopped for groceries, came over several evenings after Sy's death for prayers in our home. And if he couldn't be there, he made sure we had ten people to pray together, what Jews call a *minyan*. I so appreciated all his help until the evening when he tried to touch me.

That was the one that woke me up: an adult man, married, pretending to help and at the same time planning to assault me. It was demeaning, exhausting, and something I had never taken seriously before Sy died. But now I had to look at this reality.

Lesson #19: You cannot afford to remain naive about what it means to be an adult woman in the world as it exists today.

Looking back I see how Nan and I were almost like two teenagers together, both of us learning about dating at the same time. We would laugh together, commiserate late at night together, and became close over shared meals, conversations and everyday experiences.

CHAPTER 22
A MARRIAGE OF EQUALS: MEETING AND MARRYING SENATOR W. LOUIS COPPERSMITH

Looking at the wedding photographs of Sy and me, I can see that I was quite apprehensive. Sy has a big grin on his face, but I look tense.

For our honeymoon at the New Yorker hotel, we drove to the city followed by younger cousins who were planning to haze us on our wedding night, a tradition I'm happy to see has disappeared. We managed to lose them when we ducked off the highway at Stroudsburg and hid out for an hour or so at the Penn Stroud diner. I would have preferred staying up all night in the diner and just talking.

When we got to our hotel room, I tried hiding in the bathroom, until Sy jokingly said, "Aren't you ever coming out of there?" I considered that option, but finally went to my fate, scared as a week-old kitten. I was covered head to toe in a white silky gown with another cover up over that, a very immature twenty-year-old virgin.

***

When I started to date again in my forties, feminism had changed everything: birth control, marriage equality, our core ideas about gender and sexuality.

In April 1977, after several false starts, I had given up on the idea of finding another husband, or even a suitable date. I planned to attend the annual fundraising dinner for Pennsylvanians for Effective Government (PEG), a Republican lobbying organization, and I didn't want to drive back and forth to Hershey alone. I thought it would be a good experience for Tom Wheland, our young general manager of Morgan Signs, to attend with me. He appreciated the invitation; he even bought himself a new suit at Kalin's Men's Shop to meet the leading business folks in the Commonwealth, who were almost all middle-aged white men.

We sat up front with a group of executives from Armstrong Flooring in Lancaster. That's the first time I heard the D.C. comedy troupe Capitol Steps perform. During dinner, Tom spotted Senator W. Louis Coppersmith, a familiar face from Johnstown-Altoona television, at a nearby table and asked me if I knew him. I had met him once at an event at University House during the early part of President Oswald's tenure.

"So sad about his wife," I said, half to Tom and half to myself. Like me, Lou had lost his first spouse tragically. She had taken her own life the month before when he was running for re-election. My mind kicked into high gear, and I thought about Lou the whole way through dinner. I was unhappy on the social side of life. He was Jewish and attractive.

I mustered the nerve to go up to him at the end of the dinner.

"Senator Coppersmith," I began formally, a bit tentative, "I'm sure you don't remember, but I'm Mimi Barash, and we met at a pre-game tailgate at President Oswald's house. I want to express my condolences to you. Let me assure you the loss doesn't go away, but it does get a little better with time." I bid farewell, and Tom drove us back to State College.

On the drive home, I asked Tom, "What in the world possessed you to point out Senator Coppersmith to me?"

"I just thought you might know him," he innocently replied.

"Well, let me tell you," I confided, "I wish I knew how to get to know him better. A nice man, a good man, not a bad looking man, and Jewish—my mother would approve—and he's an attorney and a senator, too!"

The next day, I thought of the situation as a salesperson would. I asked myself, "What would Sy, the best salesperson I knew, do in this situation?" Sy might have called, but I decided, given the gender dynamics, it would be better to start by writing a letter, short and sweet.

A few days later, just as I walked into the office from a trip to DuBois to service our bank client there, Gail Patrick, our receptionist, called out, "Mrs. B, Senator Coppersmith on line three!"

I froze. Then I rushed to my office, closed the door, picked up the phone, and blurted out, "Hello, Senator Coppersmith."

He asked about the outcome of the special election for the State Senate seat opened by Joe Ammerman's election to Congress, the seat for which the Republican State Committee had targeted me. I explained how I'd lost in the nominating convention, at which Centre County Commissioner Doyle Corman threw his hat into the ring. We were discussing Doyle's landslide victory over Democrat Gilbert "Mac" McCrossin ('28), and the conversation seemed to be stuck.

"Is that all you want?" I softly asked.

"Actually, I'll be returning to Harrisburg Sunday, and I thought I could come through State College and take you to dinner. You pick the place. I'd like to get to know you." He was a man of few words, and quite direct.

My dating and ultimate marriage to Lou represents one of those amazing coincidences that can only occur through relationships. I later learned that Lou happened to be driving with another State Senator, Bobby Jubelirer ('59), to a hearing in Philadelphia the day after we ran into one another at the PEG dinner. Bobby, Lou's colleague from the other side of the aisle, was a close friend of ours from his undergraduate days at Beta Sigma Rho fraternity, where Sy was the alumni advisor. His older brother, Jim ('51), had been Sy's roommate in 1950. Lou questioned Bobby about me, mentioning our brief exchange at the dinner. Bobby suggested that Lou call me. If Lou had not been on that ride one day after our brief rendezvous, he might never have followed up, especially knowing now how absent-minded he could be and how many other women he was dating at the time.

Was it love at first sight? No. But, a remarkably affable and interesting start for two complex grownups at what they called "Mimi's Table" at the Allen Street Grill above the Corner Room. After dinner, we shook hands, and he said he'd be in touch.

It's not easy to write this because I want to smile and cry at the same time. Lou Coppersmith, complex, deeply caring, and often critical, was helpful to me in so many ways, almost immediately after that first date, which, looking back, seems quite formal and almost businesslike. But all the signs of our compatibility were there. He asked questions that made me a better business person. He suggested I make peace with my mother. He had more experience than I did in the legal side of business, but he listened, without judgment, helping me figure out things for myself.

We were both adults, with our own lives and work, but we also had so much in common: great conversation, fulfilling sex, and a kind of compatibility that I had no idea how to access in my first, very happy but also immature, marriage to Sy.

Early on, I tried to get him to talk about his first wife's depression and tragic death.

"Mimi," he said, "some things aren't worth talking about." And I did not ask about it again.

Lesson #20: With the proper timing and as a more mature adult, love really can be more beautiful the second time around.

My first marriage had lots of exploring, adjusting, and fact finding. The second time, I knew what I wanted and the terms on which I wanted it. I understood more about myself, about the nature of love, and how much more I enjoy life with a companion.

I used to say to Lou, completely in jest, "The only thing I don't love about you is you're so much more intelligent than I am." I so admired how he could see and solve a problem. I loved his training as a lawyer and experience in public office: how he set the boundaries of our discussion, explained in detail how systems work and why some things take more time, work, and compromise than others.

It's easy to understand how Lou gained his reputation as the "conscience of the Senate." His moral compass never turned off, and his ability to frame and organize debate in a way that was respectful of others became an important ingredient to my growing role as a public figure.

We often discussed how we had found one another at the right moment, and how we had made a difference for each other in so many ways. He took care of himself by eating well and exercising, but when we met he was wearing the same boring clothes he'd been wearing for a decade; he looked worn out from his personal struggles. I helped him learn to give his appearance a higher priority. He was also much closer to the wound of losing his spouse, and having had more time to recover, I helped to ease him through that recovery.

Memories of my marriage to Lou bring back only joy—from our simple wedding ceremony for close family and friends at Eisenhower Chapel, with Rabbi Jeff Eisenstat ('70) leading on his guitar, to the dinner in the Fireside Lounge at The Nittany Lion Inn.

We stayed in the Evan Pugh suite at the Inn that night. When I went to make the reservation, Bill Bohn, the general manager, referred me to Rose Oswald for final approval. Odd as the request seemed, I followed his directions. It turned out that Rose had concerns about my decision to marry Lou, who had apparently given Jack a hard time at a budget hearing in Harrisburg. Not wanting to engage in "warfare" with Rose, who had good intentions, I offered to stay elsewhere.

"No, No, you go ahead," she said. "I just want to be sure you know what you're doing."

***

Lou and I combined our families, bringing together five adult children into one blended and expanding family. We shared the joy of three weddings and the birth of three grandchildren and had so much hope for our shared future. We were so deeply blessed to have met when we did. He needed me, and I needed him, and together we helped one another get on with lives that had been broken open by loss.

1. Nan Barash, Lou Coppersmith and me at Nan's college graduation in 1983.

2. Every year, for the Sy Barash Regatta, we helped the organizers make t-shirts, buttons and signs.

3. I opened up a lot of new doors in the 1980s and 1990s. This is me at work as a Penn State trustee.

4. I switched my registration from Republican to Democrat to support Lou's re-election to the Pennsylvania state senate.

5. Bill Schreyer, chair of Merrill Lynch, was my vice chair and close advisor when I was chair of the Penn State board.

107

THE 1980s

As a result of the 1980 census, State College officially became a metropolis, with a population of 36,130. The town was more than twice the size of what it had been when I arrived in 1950. And I had come to be recognized as someone who could get things done—both in the town and at the university.

In 1980, when Lou ran for re-election to the State Senate District #35, I changed my registration from Republican to Democrat, so I could vote for him in the primary, and I have been a registered Democrat ever since. Lou lost to Mark Singel ('74) in the Democratic primary in 1980, giving us a lot more time to enjoy our marriage, which we split between homes in State College and Johnstown.

I received state and national awards in the 1980s, each one more flabbergasting than the last, since I basically still thought of myself as a small-town girl who worked hard and got things done but was not "in the big league." Governor Dick Thornburgh appointed me to the Pennsylvania Commission for Women. I was named Pennsylvania Small Business Person of the Year and Distinguished Daughter of Pennsylvania, and I also won the National Governors' Association Award for Service to State Government and was appointed to the Pennsylvania Public Television Commission. The Barash Group was honored for our philanthropic work, including by the American Cancer Society, where I stayed involved in tribute and memory to Sy. Bit by bit, I realized that the world saw me differently, and that brought me a sense of both opportunity and responsibility to help other people.

I tried to use my increased visibility to support causes I believed in. The Barash Group contributed billboard space to the League of Women Voters to encourage people to get out to vote. We also worked on a film for Trout Unlimited, a regional organization that

109

protects fish and waterways, that included President Jimmy Carter fly-fishing in Spruce Creek.

In the 1980s, both of my daughters graduated from college, and both were married. Two of Lou's children were married as well. And our first three grandchildren were born. I received (and saved) letters from many friends who had moved away from State College over the years and were considering moving back to retire.

Between 1983 and 1990, President Bryce Jordan brought a level of vigor and vitality to all parts of the university. Penn State advanced academically and athletically, winning our only two national championships in football—in 1983, we upset Georgia in the Sugar Bowl, and in 1986, we came from behind to win the Fiesta Bowl against highly-favored and poorly-behaved Miami. We joined the Big Ten in 1990.

When Bryce Jordan entered the room, he took it over. He was extremely attentive to details, the consummate leader and deal-maker. I admired his capacity for work and innovative thinking. Some of his most important contributions to the university, especially around technology and entrepreneurship, did not come to fruition until after he left Penn State.

Lesson #21: This may be the truest test of greatness: how your vision lives on when you are no longer guiding the details yourself.

Jonelle Jordan, his wife, also captured the hearts of Happy Valley. She was a gracious hostess, and for me a kind friend. She hosted a party before Carol's wedding for our out of town guests. And she made sure I knew that she appreciated my volunteer work, sending me small gifts when I worked hard and achieved important breakthroughs for the university.

My business grew dramatically in this decade. Through my work on the Penn State Board of Trustees, I met wonderful people across the university and grew into a figure of statewide prominence and visibility. In many ways, my life was everything I'd ever dreamed of—and more.

In 1987 Lou and I broke ground on a project Sy and I had dreamed about for more than twenty years: to use our block of downtown property to build a place that was set back sufficiently from the street so people could enjoy the public space, with offices and condominiums built above, including our own new home.

We had picked out all the furnishings and were about to move into The Towers when, late in the afternoon on January 17, 1989, Lou suffered a massive heart attack while running at the YMCA in downtown Johnstown. He never came home.

Recalling that day still brings tears to my eyes. As sad and horrific as it was to lose Sy, we were partially prepared by his extended decline. The utter shock of Lou's death totally undid me. When Sy died, I had two children at home, and during the early stages of grief, Nan was my constant companion. Now, my combined children and grandchildren were scattered all over the globe, and I was alone, at home, for the first time in my life.

***

On January 31, 1989, which was the thirty-fifth anniversary of my wedding to Sy Barash, and two weeks after the death of my second husband, Lou Coppersmith, I was on the brink of bankruptcy, but I insisted that we go on with the grand opening party for the new Barash Group offices in The Towers. I stood between my desk and chair for more than three hours, shaking hands and hugging hundreds of people who stopped by to share their condolences and wish me well in the future. This wave of friends and colleagues buoyed me up, and I felt for a moment, like they and I would get through.

But it got worse before it got better. In July 1989 I was in New York City for a second date with Sam Fredman ('42), a man I had known since the mid '50s from Sy's fraternity, when I discovered a lump in my breast. I was still struggling both to rent the offices and to sell the condominiums in The Towers. And all this time I never once talked to a therapist. I was still facing the world as something I was supposed to conquer with my own boundless stamina and good sense. I went back to the feeling I had when my brother died in World War II: that I was meant to take this in, that I was to learn from it, that I was meant to use my personal experience of pain as a way to make the world a bit better for other people.

CHAPTER 23
THE VALUE OF YOUR WORK: PICK ME UP BOUQUETS

In the early 1980s, a unique piece of business came our way through agency work with Bloomsburg Bank. The bank was a long-standing client; their board chair, Douglas Dillon, was president of Dillon Flowers, a family-owned wholesale rose growing company in Bloomsburg since 1875.

Dillon came to my office to discuss a business challenge.

He explained, "There are major changes on the horizon for the retail side of the cut flower business." He spoke quietly, as if letting me in on a secret: "No longer will cut flowers be sold exclusively in retail flower and gift shops. People will buy flowers in places they already shop, like supermarkets and department stores." To stay ahead of that shift, he would need to sell flowers directly through supermarkets and other retail establishments, in addition to floral shops.

His asked us to create a catchy name for a new product, one that could be connected directly to customers through this new channel, complete with graphics that would provide solid branding for a successful launch. This was the kind of challenge I loved.

He said, "Just give me some ideas. I don't want to spend a lot of money."

In my enthusiasm to close the sale, I did something you should almost never do in business. I should have asked, "What is not a lot of money?" But I answered from my gut, "We could do the initial phase—names and graphic concepts—for somewhere between $1200 and $1500."

"That's perfect," he said.

As was my custom, I gathered all the "thinkers" from different parts of The Barash Group for a brainstorming session in my corner office. We sat at the round, Lucite table in front of my cluttered desk and began a well-established process. There were four of us: Jo Chesworth, a writer; Witt Yeagley, the editor of *Town & Gown*; Ron Shroyer, our Creative Director; and me. It was one of those times when everything just clicked. Ideas flowed quickly. We were laughing and joking and almost immediately zeroed in on one concept that seemed to capture what they were looking for: a reason to buy flowers, on a whim, at a place where you didn't expect to see them.

I lifted up my arms, leaned back in my chair, and said, "I've got it. Pick Me Up flowers!"

We were all high-fiving our big idea: "Pick Me Up" flowers, with the double meaning of how easy it was to grab and go, and the deeper sense of fresh flowers improving people's spirits. With less than half an hour of brainstorming, we were off and running. We delivered the job early, creating a full mockup of the concept for Pick Me Up Bouquets complete with a rainbow design.

Always committed to fairness, we billed Dillon Flowers $1200 for the full-blown concept that had evolved so quickly. We released the work to him and provided him with the forms to copyright the name and design.

Imagine my surprise on my commute from Johnstown to State College about a year later, when I stopped at a red light on Route 220 coming into Altoona and saw a sign in a local floral shop, for a "Pick Me Up bouquet." It was our design, plain and simple. I couldn't wait to find out what happened.

Next time we made our monthly visit to clients in Bloomsburg, I told Doug Dillon about the coincidence and asked him if he knew about it. He told me that FTD had paid them to "cease and desist" from using the name, so FTD could trademark it. I never had the guts to ask him how much he made on that deal, but if I'd made even a penny on every time that idea was used by FTD, I'd have made thousands off that deal and still be making more.

I hadn't yet learned to look beyond the time spent on a job to the actual value of the work to the customer. In general, I feel that many women tend to undervalue our services in this way.

Lesson #22: Define value in terms of what it's worth to your customer, rather than always billing for hours, as if you're a tradesperson or service worker. You are probably worth more than you think.

It was interesting, too, that the concept we created for flower sales outside of floral shops became a mainstay for those good, old-fashioned retail floral shops. Sales of flowers, both in and out of florists, benefitted from the "grab and go" concept we helped to accelerate into the world.

CHAPTER 24
THE POWER OF VOLUNTEER LEADERSHIP: THE CENTRE COMMUNITY FOUNDATION

When Judge R. Paul Campbell ('30) retired from the Centre County Court of Common Pleas after over twenty years of service, he devoted his time to starting a foundation to benefit nonprofits in Centre County. I was honored to be among the local leaders he brought together to develop and initiate a start-up plan. Sy and I had developed a friendship with Judge Campbell during one of his re-election bids. When Sy died, I made a conscious effort to keep up this network of influential community leaders.

Lesson #23: Stay connected with the people who make things happen in your community. If you have the chance to serve in your local community foundation—or to start a new local philanthropy—don't be afraid to say yes.

There is no part of your life that won't benefit from engagement with your local community, even when it takes you a bit out of your usual comfort zone.

Before becoming a judge, Campbell had served as an estate attorney, and he returned to that work after he retired. He had many wealthy friends and clients looking for a vehicle to support local nonprofits. As a judge he had seen many young people who got in trouble early in life and never quite recovered. He wanted both to open up an avenue for his friends and clients to give back to the local community and to leave a legacy of helping those troubled young people whom he ran into as a judge and was unable to help, on multiple occasions, once they were already entangled in the legal system.

In 1981, we officially launched the foundation, really just a shell at the time, for people to create endowments to support causes they believed in. A designated fund to support the American Red Cross got the foundation off the ground. When Campbell decided to step down as our Foundation leader, he asked me to succeed him as President from 1986 to 1989. He thought of it very much as his organization and retained all the records. If I needed anything for reference or continuity, I had to request the material from him.

Was I insulted? Yes! This setup went very much against my usual drive to be in charge, but I did it out of respect for Judge Campbell and, honestly, because I felt I had to. Things were changing in our community, but it was still unusual for a woman to lead locally. I felt it was more important to do the essential work to grow the Foundation than to fight for more visible control.

This was a big breakthrough for me: I felt confident enough that I just did the work. I knew it wasn't about me; it was about what I could do for our community for the long run. Most importantly, I expanded the Foundation beyond a small group of insiders, adding people to the board who would become the next generation of leadership. And, quietly but persistently, I encouraged women to give money to the Foundation and direct their gifts to the Women's Resource Center, addressing the needs of sexually abused and assaulted women and children long before that problem was recognized in most small-town communities.

With the name change to the Centre Foundation in 2013 and the addition of Centre Gives, an annual 36-hour online fundraising marathon, the Foundation now raises over $1 million annually benefiting scores of local organizations and individuals. Today, there are nearly 500 different funds totaling over $38 million and providing grants of over $18 million annually. Some of the largest endowments support the Schlow Library, Meals on Wheels, Women's Resource Center, Arts Festival, and Youth Service Bureau, which was Campbell's personal mission.

Happily, the Foundation's spirit for philanthropy touched—and continues to touch--young people. Today, high school students can participate directly in the philanthropic process through Centre PACT (Philanthropic Actions Created by Teens), a program that encourages students to develop their own programs and participate in the grant process.

I fondly remember getting Penn State students on board the local philanthropy train as a student in the early '50s. The Community Chest was my first foray into supporting the local community. And, in the early 1960s, when the Community Chest was on the brink of death, from a volunteer treasurer who had embezzled funds, I was one of a small group of people who helped to rescue it.

So I proudly watched as the State College Community Chest grew into the United Fund and later the United Way. In the early 2000s, I was able to become a major donor and advisor to the United Way, but that type of "all begs in one ask-it" is not the future direction of philanthropy. The Centre Foundation, embedded in a broad range of community needs and individuals' unique commitments and ways of giving, is much more consistent with the direction philanthropy is moving.

CHAPTER 25
KNOW WHEN TO STOP: MY PURCHASE OF DUBOIS OUTDOOR

As the '80s progressed, I began to expand the billboard business beyond our original footprint. One day, out of the clear blue, an old friend from Penn State, Marc Katzen ('61), called me. Sy and I had managed his first campaign for County Commissioner in 1968. He had won, as the youngest person and first Jewish person elected to a county office in Jefferson County.

Marc was calling to see if I had any interest in buying a small inventory of billboards in the greater DuBois area. DuBois Outdoor was owned by the Way family, with the sole survivor getting up in age and suffering from complications of alcoholism.

"I'm always willing to take a look," I replied.

I sent Dick Hall, my seasoned general manager, to inspect the condition of their billboard plant. The boards were in a horrible state and needed a tremendous amount of repair. When I called Marc back, he asked for $50,000. I declined.

He kept coming back to me, and I finally agreed to purchase DuBois Outdoor for $28,000 cash.

When I tried to chisel a little more, at the very end, Marc reminded me, "Mimi, Sy once told me not to squeeze the last nickel out of every deal." I smiled and agreed with him.

Lesson #24: Negotiating is good, but don't negotiate yourself out of a deal.

The big bonus on this purchase was one of my most loyal employees ever. Doyle Duttry, a bill poster, never stops thanking me for the opportunities for professional growth he had while employed by Morgan Signs and the secure retirement provided by our benefits package. Of hundreds of employees over the years, most of whom received the same benefits, he is one of very few who continue to stay in touch with me. Doyle and his wife Norma send me a card for every Jewish holiday.

Lesson #25: Just like an employee, the boss also gets a lift when people thank them for a job well done. Consider it sometime; it rarely happens and is deeply appreciated and long remembered.

CHAPTER 26
MOVE SWIFTLY ON A BUSINESS IMPERATIVE: THE MEADOWS INTERSECTION

Like the fast food business, billboards located at the intersection of two major roads attract the most attention. I had always been aggressive in securing the most desirable billboard locations throughout our territory. We had leased the open land at the Meadows Intersection, at the crossing of Routes 36 and 220 in Duncanville, and placed four boards (two large billboards and two smaller ones) in plain view from both directions.

Pittsburgh Outdoor eyed the property for possible purchase when a "For Sale" sign appeared on the property, offered by W. W. Wilt in Altoona.

Tom Wheland, who was with me the night I spoke with Lou at the Pennsylvanians for Effective Government dinner in Hershey, had jumped ship suddenly a year later, and gone to work for Pittsburgh Outdoor's Mid-State, our biggest competitor. My billboard foreman, Joe Hofer, called to report that he'd seen Tom at the Meadows Intersection site, and Tom had bragged, "Now she'll have to talk to me!"

My competitor's attempt to steal my location, led by a former employee, was a strong ethical transgression in the billboard business, and it made me furious.

As soon as I got off the phone with Joe, I ran upstairs to the accounting department to review our Meadows Intersection lease. I looked for the clause, "In the event that property is offered for sale, lessee has first right of refusal for purchase."

I danced downstairs to my office and called Mr. Wilt. I introduced myself as the owner of Morgan Signs and asked about purchasing the plot on which I held the lease.

He quickly replied, "I'm sorry, but it's under contract."

I went on, "How much is it?"

"$30,000," he said.

"Well, Mr. Wilt, I'd like to purchase it," I continued.

"As I mentioned earlier, it's under contract," he retorted.

"Has any money exchanged hands?"

"No," he told me.

"Well, as I said, I'd like to purchase it. Let me read you a clause from my signed lease."

Then I read my good news. There was dead silence for about fifteen seconds, then he replied, "Sounds like you may be able to buy it."

"I'll tell you what, Mr. Wilt, to underscore my intent, I'll send you a $500 deposit today, and you can draw up the agreement of sale."

I was ecstatic through those exhilarating moments. I called Lou. Lou had suggested that we simplify our billboard leases, eliminating the old-fashioned right to purchase clause. I disagreed with Lou on that one because some lessors gave us that right, and sometimes we exercised it.

"How can you offer that kind of money without a formal appraisal?" Lou confronted me.

"If it's worth that to Mid-State, it's certainly worth it to me," I explained. I was still high on adrenaline.

"Be sure you don't overreact," Lou warned me and then offered, "I'll take a look at the property on my way to State College for the weekend and let you know if I have further thoughts."

"Lou, it doesn't matter," I explained. "Worth it or not, this move will help Mid-State understand they can't play dirty with us."

"Maybe... it's just business, Mimi. I'll check it out."

After Lou looked at the property himself, he offered to go into the deal with me 50-50. In the end, I made the purchase personally, and my company signed a new lease with me.

When I began to experience excruciating financial challenges a few years later, I sold the Meadows Intersection to the adjacent property owner, with a permanent easement to keep my billboards there. That deal brought in $125,000, enough to meet nearly three monthly interest payments on my construction loan and to put off the inevitable workout with the bank until almost a year later.

In the end, Mid-State and Morgan were both purchased by

Lamar Advertising. But my ability to move swiftly and my fierce insistence that my larger business competitors—almost always male—take me seriously, and my refusal to roll over and play dead when they tried to push me around, drove up the value of my business throughout the '80s and '90s, and helped me to retire comfortably.

Lesson #26: Insist on being taken seriously, no matter your audience, no matter your odds.

CHAPTER 27
BREAKING THROUGH: VICE CHAIR, PENN STATE BOARD OF TRUSTEES

The process for selecting Penn State's trustees is extremely political, rather convoluted, and even today less than fully transparent. The governor appoints six trustees, four ex officio (meaning, "by virtue of their role" in state government) and two others approved by the State Senate. Three trustees each are appointed by committees representing Pennsylvania agricultural and industrial organizations (they are commonly referred to as the "agriculture" and " industrial" trustees), and nine are elected by members of the Penn State Alumni Association. The immediate past president of the Alumni Association and a student trustee round out the board of thirty-eight.

When Helen Dickerson Wise, the first woman elected by alumni to the Penn State Board of Trustees in 1969, lost her bid to become vice chair in January 1985 by a 15-13 vote favoring agriculture trustee Obie Snider ('40), industrial trustee Mike Beaver, leaned over and whispered to me, "I couldn't vote for her, but I would vote for you."

That notion was completely foreign to me. I had worked hard on Helen's behalf. I felt bad for her and even worse because it was a rare opportunity to advance the status of women at the highest volunteer level at Penn State. We lost a great opportunity to break the barrier. But that loss planted a seed, and I began to nurture my sense of responsibility as a woman to expand my influence and leadership.

Lesson #27: Just because it hasn't happened before doesn't mean that it can't ever happen. You can be an influence and a leader. It's your responsibility to the future that you try.

I determined that day to do everything I could to become the first woman chair of the Penn State Board of Trustees.

My response to Mike: "I may be back to you in three years and ask you to place my name in nomination. Stay tuned."

That day arrived in January 1987, during a heavy snowstorm, which could have cost me the election. Richard Trumka ('71), a gubernatorial appointee, had scheduled his flight from Washington, D.C., during a break from labor union negotiations for the AFL-CIO. He was scheduled to arrive at 10:00 a.m., the exact same time the vote for new board officers would take place in the Trustee Meeting Room on the second floor of the Keller Building.

As I watched the snow accumulate out the window, I couldn't help thinking that I had come so close to this dream. I wondered whether all my hard work building a coalition was going to be lost to the weather. I was reminded just how much in life you cannot control.

For months, I had been counting my votes and building support, one trustee at a time. If Trumka arrived in time, I would win the landmark election, 15-14. If he didn't arrive in time, votes would be tied. Rules required that in the event of a tie, the chairman breaks the tie. In that case, I was doomed to lose, by the same vote. I felt such a sense of relief when Trumka came through the door, just minutes before the vote, kicking his boots to remove the snow. The rest of that day is a blur of joy and achievement for me.

The turning point of my campaign strategy had come from Lou, who provided strategic direction and plain old political savvy as I considered my run for vice chair. A former officer of the board, whom I considered a good friend, called me regularly and asked me how my campaign was coming along. Naïve as I was, I openly kept him up-to-date on my progress.

Lou insisted, "Don't tell him too much. He could be working for your opponent," a very nice member of the legislature from "God's country" in northern Pennsylvania. "One way to check," Lou suggested. "Call the student trustee and fill her in about your doubt. If the trustee who keeps calling you for an update happens to call her, ask her to express some doubt about you, just enough to get him on another path. If he doesn't call her, you've lost nothing."

I took his advice. The former officer called the student trustee, and never said a word about it on his next call to me. After that, I made a point to politely but persistently avoid his calls.

There was a "gentleman's agreement" that board officers would serve for three years but needed to be re-elected by the board annually. This allowed the old guard to maintain a fierce hold on the status quo, even after we had made the overall governance of the board more transparent to the outside world.

My first year as vice chair I spent learning the ropes and doing everything extremely conventionally. My sturdy and reliable performance in that first year as vice chair made my re-election for year two inevitable. The second year of my term as vice chair brought new responsibilities and the opportunity to work closely and collaboratively with Industrial trustee and board chair, Lloyd Huck ('43). In January 1990, I was elected for the third year of my term as vice chair, but there were signs of trouble afoot with eight trustees abstaining from the vote.

Meanwhile, quietly and steadily behind the scenes, I worked to build momentum for my try at the board chair. Before the March board meeting at Hershey Medical Center in 1990, Huck called me unexpectedly to the chairman's suite. He alerted me that the eight trustees who had abstained on my re-election vote were planning to oppose my future nomination as chair.

He said, bluntly, "They feel your personality doesn't suit the role and responsibility of the chair of the board." They were also concerned that there was a conflict of interest between my business and my potential role as board chair.

I had prepared mentally for just this moment, steeled myself, and asked Lloyd, "Would you really want to be the person who broke 'tradition' to help stop a woman from assuming leadership? Is there anything other than my so-called temperament that should deny me the opportunity?"

He said he knew me to be responsible and committed to our alma mater. While my sex, religion, and liberal politics represented a new vision on tough issues that was hard for some on the board to digest, he assured me that he would not break tradition. But he said he could not protect me against someone else entering the race in opposition.

Penn State alum and industrial trustee William "Bill" Schreyer ('48) was that person. Bill, who would occasionally hint that he was getting close to retirement as chair of Merrill Lynch, was an obvious candidate to be board chair in the future. White, male, charismatic, and with a national reputation in the finance industry, he would be solidly backed by everyone, especially the conservative men who dominated the board.

I refused to give up. However, as much as I wanted to win, I did not want to be elected chair on a split decision, which would ultimately hamper my ability to get work done as chair. I set up a meeting with Schreyer to bring him up to speed on the election, in case he didn't already know. He explained that the dissidents had asked him to join in the move to defeat me or discourage me from seeking the chairmanship, and he had declined.

Together, we agreed that he would seek the vice chairmanship on a ticket that had me as candidate for chair. At the same time, I asked him, based on his individual plans, when he hoped to seek the chairmanship. He said, ideally, in two years, after the second year of my chairmanship. I offered to break the tradition of three one-year terms for officers and accept two one-year terms as chair. This compromise enabled me to break the glass ceiling, appease my opposition, and give Schreyer what he needed to accept my candidacy wholeheartedly. And, when the time came, the vote was unanimous!

Lesson #28: Seeking consensus is a key component of effective leadership, and one that can require practice for those of us to whom it doesn't come naturally.

Between the call-to-action to become president of the chamber of commerce in 1973 and my election as the first woman chair of the Penn State Board of Trustees in 1990, I learned how to listen to all sides of a discussion and to work to achieve my goals without alienating people whose positions were different from my own.

Frankly, I've never learned a thing on those days when everything fell into place. It's the challenging days that have taught me how to cope, how to maintain my character and integrity, how to get up, brush myself off, and start all over again. My experience as a public figure in a vibrant university community taught me how to learn from my critics, to understand different points of view, and move in new directions when you hold positions of power, being strong as well as fair.

126

In two years as chair of the Penn State board, I was able to lead several key initiatives, including the expansion of the airport, so we could bring more commercial air service to University Park—an initiative I'd started as president of the chamber of commerce during Sy's illness.

My moment of historical significance came when our board found the courage and strength to add gay, lesbian, transgender, and bisexual rights to the university's nondiscrimination policy by a vote of 17 to 10 in 1991. That took a collaborative effort by President Joab Thomas, board vice chair Bill Schreyer ('48), and me to take the message personally to each trustee and make the case for equal rights and fair treatment, according to the U.S. Constitution and the Pennsylvania Declaration of Rights.

This is also the achievement for which I am most criticized by conservatives. After it passed, there were letters in the *Penn Stater* that tried to shoot us down, and I personally received a couple really nasty, unsigned letters as well. I learned that in order to lead you need to be able to withstand backlash on particularly sensitive issues.

***

There are other funny things I remember: every board chair before me had the option to fly with the team to all away football games, but I was told that wasn't an option.

"Not even the coaches' wives go on the team plane," was how the news was broken to me at the time.

Through my entire journey on the Penn State board, whenever I was confused about what was going on at the university or frustrated that I could not change things as quickly as I wanted to, or provide the kind of leadership I imagined because my hands were tied, my go-to person at the university was Carol Herrmann ('70), Senior Vice President for Administration. To this day, we jokingly refer to those sensitive conversations as "holding hands." Without her strategic suggestions and calming advice at key moments, I would have blundered far more often. This was an example of how I was able to work both the traditional power structure, which was still mostly male, and the informal networks, behind the scenes, where women had less power officially, but a lot more information and influence than we sometimes let on.

127

Since my chairmanship, two other women have been elected board chair, and neither was contested on the basis of gender. The Penn State board has become much more transparent and democratic over the past thirty years, but it has also become more fractious, as has come to light in recent years over the Sandusky and Paterno controversies, in a direction that makes the board nearly ungovernable. But that is a story for another day.

CHAPTER 28
NO WORDS: LOSING LOU COPPERSMITH

Late afternoon, January 17, 1989. I was driving home from the grocery store to my Toftrees apartment, where I moved after the house on Homan Avenue was burglarized while I was on vacation. I had a big cell phone in my car. It rang, and when I answered I heard the voice of Lou's cousin, Paul Glosser, telling me, "You need to come to Johnstown. Lou had a heart attack while running and is in Johnstown Hospital in critical condition."

How could I make that drive alone under those conditions? The only person I could think of to drive me was Mike Snook, who worked in our accounting department at night. He dropped what he was doing, picked me up at my apartment where I threw all the groceries in the refrigerator. I was about to make dinner for our general manager, Pat Rosdil, that night. She was planning to tell me she intended to return to Penn State to work, the first of many crushing blows I experienced in the midst of my grief.

From the car, I kept calling the Johnstown Hospital, with no success. Finally, the rabbi picked up the phone at the hospital.

"I'm so sorry, Mimi..." he began.

***

While everyone was together in Johnstown, telling stories and chasing babies around the house, it was as if Lou was present in our shared memories and rituals. There are really no words for how forlorn I felt when all the Barash and Coppersmith children and grandchildren went back home after Lou's funeral.

I had never been alone like this—living alone, eating alone, alone with my own sad thoughts—and I hated it. Lou was not only a wonderful partner and friend, he was also my trusted business advisor. There was no part of my life he had not shared and made better.

Lou was a man of few words, but when he spoke, people listened. I frequently quote him on taxes, "The only thing worse than paying taxes is not having to," and marriage, "the nicest part of being angry is making up."

Lou's father had died at age fifty-six of a heart attack, and a few years before Lou's death, we were warned that, like his father, he had silent ischemia. We went to Cleveland Clinic, where they diagnosed Lou's condition and treated it with angioplasty. We were sent away quite hopeful. He seemed so healthy, tall and thin. He loved the outdoors, and his skin was tan. He watched what he ate and exercised religiously, including daily runs. He was the perfect partner and brought out the best in me. And then he was gone.

The hardest part was the loss of his sage advice and tender, loving help. It felt like we could solve anything together. How could I continue without him? His death left such a big hole in my heart and daily life. My work became my therapy: I needed to make sure I could meet the payroll for fifty employees. But more than that, I worked to stave off despair.

I went with the Palmers to Grand Cayman and started the writing that ultimately became this book. But the writing took me back to a well of pain and loss: my brother, my father, my sister, and now two husbands. I was haunted by memories of fighting bitterly with my mother as a child. There were times I considered ending my own life—and once I even thought of a plan—but there was something in my makeup, something in my sense of life and purpose, that kept me going.

People from all walks of life reached out with small acts of support and love to help me over the devastating loss of Lou Coppersmith. When Sy died, I responded to every one of them individually. That was part of my recovery the first time. But this time I received so many moving cards and simple, kind gestures that I wrote one overall thank you letter to everyone, trying to define—for them, but also for myself—how this horror had meaning: what it meant to survive and adjust to overwhelming grief.

***

Quite miraculously, just a few months before Lou died, our children managed to pull off a tenth anniversary celebration for us in Philadelphia. These are the last photographs we all have together and are a reminder to grab the good things in life, because you never know what's around the corner.

CHAPTER 29
WHEN YOUR BODY CRIES, LISTEN: MY BATTLE WITH BREAST CANCER

In the midst of blistering setbacks, I received an invitation to attend the swearing in ceremony for Sam Fredman, Sy's fraternity brother, as Judge of the Supreme Court of New York, 2nd Division, in White Plains. Sam, ten years my senior, was a retired matrimonial lawyer from Westchester County. He had been appointed by Governor Mario Cuomo to serve until the results of a November general election. Sam's wife, Mims, had died in a tragic car accident in Copenhagen while they were vacationing in June 1988. I regretfully declined the invitation and advised Sam of Lou's death. In his letter of response, he sent me a copy of the letter I had written to him after learning of his wife's passing and suggested that we get together.

At that time, The Towers project was causing me big-time stress. In addition, a Faculty Senate member, Robert Heinsohn, raised a conflict of interest issue in my negotiations to lease some of the commercial space in The Towers to the university. Simultaneously, I was taking a beating in the local media: it felt like whenever I turned on local radio or TV or opened the *Centre Daily Times*, someone was talking about me in a negative light.

No one else was pursuing me in 1989, and the reappearance of someone I'd known for so long, someone I'd run into with Lou in New York just a year before, felt like a great adventure, perhaps even something that was "bashert," Yiddish for something that is "meant to be."

When Sam arrived in State College for our first date, he parked at The Towers, and I went downstairs to meet him. He was waiting beside his tan, chauffeur-driven Cadillac, quite overweight, clothed in wrinkled Penn State shorts and a Hawaiian print shirt that didn't match.

132

When I told him I had made reservations for him at the Atherton Hotel, a short walk from The Towers, he objected. "I came to stay with you," he said.

This went against everything I believed in. We had known one another for years, but this was our first "date." He promised he wouldn't hurt me. Though I felt I would never be able to tell my mother, or my closest friends, I succumbed. That's how my third marriage started. There was no courtship; it was all very matter-of-fact.

My first impression? He was kind, lonely, and interested in a serious relationship. I was the same, and nothing better had presented itself.

We had a good time over the weekend. We had so much shared past through Penn State, and, of course, heads turned when we walked through town together. Yes, we slept together, but there was no sex.

As he was leaving, he sat me down and said, "I didn't just come here for the weekend. I really think we could have a good life together."

"We don't even know one another," I responded. "Let's try getting to know one another first." We agreed to a routine that would bring us together every couple weeks to see whether something more was possible. We planned a second date, this time in New York City.

***

When my plane landed at LaGuardia, my bag was lost. Rushing to leave State College, I had packed my jewelry in my suitcase, so I was in a tizzy. With so much unsettled in every aspect of my life, I didn't know how I could cheer up and be normal for this date, especially if my bag didn't appear before show time. Exhausted as I was, physically and mentally, I decided to nap, to escape from my troubles and recover for the weekend ahead.

The phone woke me around four. US Air was delivering my bag that afternoon. I rested a little longer, and when I sat up to shower and get ready, it felt like I'd rolled over an object on the bed. I looked down and found nothing. I touched my left breast on the spot where I had felt the object. There was a lump, as big as my thumb. I was scared beyond description. Before getting up, I contorted my body in every possible direction, searching for a position where it would disappear. I sat up straight, took a number of deep breaths, and vowed

133

I'd keep my secret to myself, pull things together, and enjoy the weekend. I'd figure out what to do next on Monday.

I decided to go on with life as usual until I had my annual checkup with my gynecologist, Chuck Rohrbeck ('54), a couple weeks later. I was scheduled to spend five days with Penn State Executive Vice President and Provost Bill Richardson and his wife, Nancy, at their island home off the coast off Seattle. That provided another excuse to put my possible troubles on the shelf until after vacation and my visit to the doctor.

As always, Chuck demonstrated his caring disposition. He grew up in State College, and we met as classmates at Penn State. We chatted at first and then discussed my last check-up, where he found a suspicious area on my mammogram that we wanted to watch. I had assumed that situation reared its ugly head again.

"But that was the right breast," he reminded me.

I had another mammogram and another day of waiting. Chuck called me the next morning.

"Mimi," he said, "I'm so sorry to convey bad news by phone, but you need to see a surgeon. It appears that you have a malignancy in your left breast. The suspicious area on the right remains, but no change, so no need to worry about that."

He asked what he could do to help. I had decided before any test results that I would seek treatment at Penn State's Hershey Medical Center, a teaching hospital where they had broad experience treating and researching breast cancer. He understood my choice and helped me get a copy of the mammograms to take with me.

My next call, before I'd even stood up from my desk, went to Penn State President Bryce Jordan. In tears, I shared my news and asked if he could help facilitate an appointment with the right person at Hershey as soon as possible.

"I'm frantic," I explained. "I'm having trouble figuring out what to do next."

Bryce called back in less than an hour. He had arranged for a university plane to fly me to Harrisburg the next morning at 8:00 a.m.

"A Penn State driver will meet you at the Harrisburg airport," he said. "You'll be escorted through the Medical Center with a navigator who will accompany you through the procedures necessary to determine next steps. The university plane will return you to State

College later that afternoon." That service from the university was such a godsend.

"Oy vey," I repeated my mother's Yiddish cry of despair. Once I had the news, I was really having trouble putting one foot in front of the other. I needed to call my daughters; I had to pull things together for my employees; I couldn't stop crying or worrying.

"Pull yourself together," I spoke out loud to myself. "Mimi! Stop crying! It won't help! Call Barb."

Of course, Barb Palmer insisted on coming with me to Hershey without my even asking, just as she had been with me through Sy's long trips to Sloan Kettering almost twenty years before. Friends like Barb do what they have to do when they know they have to. That is the blessing of true friendship. Barb also reinforced my decision to bring my daughters into the loop. My secret needed to become a part of their reality as well. Nan, who by then was a key employee of The Barash Group and lived just an hour from Hershey, decided to meet us there. Carol was on a National Endowment for the Humanities fellowship at the Huntington Library in San Marino, California, with a son who had just turned a year old, so we promised to update her as soon as we had test results or other news.

I didn't talk much on that flight to Hershey in the Penn State plane. I tried to quiet my anxiety and my first, perplexing thoughts about my own mortality. I was fifty-six, and thoughts of Sy's nearly three-year struggle and untimely death loomed before me. I recalled the things I'd told myself to get through after Sy died: "Forget about self-pity. Look at this as another possible setback that you'll be able to handle." I drifted in and out of sleep, thinking, "It isn't the end of the world... you will survive... you have too much left to do. Hang in there."

The whole thing was so hard. But I was truly blessed when Nancy Toth, Hershey's top breast cancer navigator, met me at the front door to the medical center. Though she was a few years younger than me, she became like my surrogate mother, guiding me through the tests and soothing my fevered and frantic emotions. What a gift to have someone who not only takes you to every test, but also explains in detail what's happening and listens to whatever you need to say. I have only beautiful memories of that entire process because of her ability to balance scientific knowledge and empathy. She nurtured my inner strength to persevere, overcome adversity, and conquer each challenge as it came.

Lesson #29: No one can overcome adversity alone. You need to trust your instincts while also seeking external support, others who believe in you and your ability to do whatever you need to do.

In those brief hours at Hershey, I made myself ready for any news. At the end of the day, there was both bad news and good news.

"You have a malignant tumor, very early stages, in your left breast," I was told. "The suspicious area in the right breast will be biopsied when we take care of left breast, but we believe that will be negative."

I scheduled surgery for a week later, August 22, 1989, which gave me time to prepare everyone and for Carol to fly east for my surgery. Nancy counseled me to think about whether I preferred a mastectomy or a lumpectomy because the choice was mine—as it should be for all parts of a woman's body. She urged me to take a few days and think about it.

"I don't need to," I responded, "they can take the breast. I'll feel better, emotionally, when the whole thing is removed. And with modern prostheses, my vanity is safe!" It was a good sign that I was joking.

The really weird, but important, part of the reality came when Nancy escorted me into the small room where she photographed my breasts from all angles. She gave the pictures to me to have as I thought about my final decisions and the possibility of reconstructive surgery. I was someone who never wore makeup or nail polish. I'd only ever colored my hair once, in the mid 1960s and hated it. So the idea of a fake breast or a reconstructed breast was completely foreign to me. I still have those pictures tucked under a pile of bras in my underwear drawer, and I look at them from time to time.

When the day for surgery arrived, I had come to a point of strength and confidence as a result of the outcry of support and love from all directions.

Lesson #30: You can often feel others' love most of all when you're down, if you only look for it. The ability of others to pull you up seems, in a way, a touch of divinity.

Though no one said exactly these words, my conversations with others helped me understand that this challenge was meant to help me be strong in the most important way: my attitude. I had to believe I could win this battle, as so many others had. I felt strong because so many others thought of me as strong, as a fighter, a survivor, as someone who believed she could.

I signed a consent that if they found cancer in the second breast, they could take that one as well, and went into surgery with both Carol and Nan by my side. I came out with two drains in my left breast, and the tenacity to do whatever it took to recover. Carol came back with me to State College and helped me get started with my new routines. Nan came soon after Carol left. She remembers helping me do arm exercises in the shower to regain strength in my arms. I was living in my new condominium in The Towers, and since my condo was a thirty-second elevator ride to or from my office, during my recovery, I had projects delivered for me to work on at home.

As it turned out, I had the best breast cancer prognosis one could have: I was post-menopause, the cancer had not spread to my lymph nodes, and the tumor was estrogen-receptor positive, meaning it could be treated with Tamoxifen, a very mild chemotherapy that was given to many breast cancer patients after surgery, then and now. I remained on Tamoxifen for seven years.

I began to walk at least thirty minutes a day to build my energy level and to recover my zest for daily life. The walks, mostly in the morning, helped me clear my mind and think through the three major challenges I faced: keeping my business running and growing; returning to my roles in public service, especially as vice chair of the Penn State Board of Trustees; and dealing honestly with the financial crush of The Towers, which if I didn't deal with quickly would push me into bankruptcy.

1. This party to open the new Barash Group office at The Towers was held two weeks after Lou died.

2. Lou's son Sam Coppersmith visited me at The Towers, with his wife Beth Schermer, and their children, just a few months after Lou died.

3. A photo of me as Chair of the Penn State Board with former Chair Lloyd Huck and President Joab Thomas.

4. Joe Paterno was a close friend and business advisor for several decades.

5. Like mother, like daughters...Nan and Carol at Carol's home when they both worked for me.

139

THE 1990s

On February 24, 1990, I married Sam Fredman and began seventeen years of commuting back and forth between State College and Rye Brook, New York. We enjoyed the births of four more grandchildren across our combined families and celebrated many happy family events together. In that sense, the marriage was something I dearly loved and longed for.

A few months after I married Sam, I completed my workout with State College Federal Savings to salvage The Towers, and I began to get back on my own two feet financially and emotionally. In retrospect, the order of things here was backward: the marriage started with me in a fragile and dependent state, just beginning to recover from the loss of Lou, the trauma of breast cancer, and my sense of failure from the financial catastrophe of The Towers. This lack of equal footing was one of many reasons my marriage to Sam was doomed to failure from the start.

Reflecting on the early 1990s, I was obviously depressed. It boggles my mind that I continued to refuse psychiatric help and insisted on getting through on my own. I was trying to be superwoman, juggling work and family, while at the same time refusing to meet, head on, growing rifts in my personal life.

In May 1990, just before Mother's Day, my mother died after a brief illness at age eighty-eight. Happily, by that point, with Lou's help before he died, I had made peace with her.

My mother called me a few days before she died and said, "I've talked to God, and I've talked to my rabbi. I'm ready." Carol and I drove together to say goodbye to her on a rainy Friday morning. When we arrived, Nan was already there. Nan remembers that my mother had already passed when Carol and I arrived. Carol remembers seeing her right before she died. And I can't remember that day at all. Nan had visited her earlier that week, to bring her pictures of a new grandchild and make sure she had left nothing valuable in her federally subsidized senior citizens apartment. Nan found over $8000 hidden in her grandmother's dresser drawers in $20 and $50 bills.

My mother had been widowed since 1956, when she was fifty-five. She went back to work after her husband died so she could take care of herself and put my brother Sandy through Harvard. My mother adored both Sy and Lou, and accepted Sam with this backhanded warning: "I never interfere with my children... unless it's necessary." She meant no wrong by this statement; it was just the blunt and unpolished way she spoke. She loved him and was so happy for my third marriage, but there was another part of her that didn't entirely trust him. When I am confused and doubt myself, I often hear my mother's voice and feel tremendous gratitude for all I learned from her.

***

Sam liked to call me "the bridge" between State College and Penn State. He enjoyed not only my success, but also all the parties, awards, and socializing that had become part of my life by this time. The many opportunities in the 1990s to help make things happen within and between State College and Penn State gave me a sense of active citizenship at the highest level. Many people depended on me—from sexually abused women who came to me for advice to strangers who needed help getting back on their feet financially. People understood me to be a problem-solver, someone who could get things done. This felt very good and was part of my overall healing and appreciation of all that life had given me, from that time until today.

I rode the wave of national visibility and steady growth at Penn State and in State College throughout the decade. In 1991, a year after Penn State joined the Big Ten and the same year I was elected the first woman and the first (and only) Jewish chair of the Penn State Board of Trustees, Shaner and Associates, a large, national hotel owner and operator, relocated their headquarters and leadership team from Olean, New York, to State College. They were looking for an up-and-coming college town, and in the end, State College beat out

Chapel Hill, North Carolina, home to the University of North Carolina Tar Heels.

I later served on a committee that worked with the town and university to attract the Pittsburgh Symphony Orchestra to summer in State College, patterned on the relationship between the Boston Symphony and the western Massachusetts town of Tanglewood. Although the Pittsburgh Symphony decided to stay in Pittsburgh for the summer, the collaborative effort to complete that proposal showed many of us in the local community how much we had to offer the world as a college town and as a regional leader in education, the arts, technology, and business innovation.

During my term as vice chair and then chair of the Penn State Board of Trustees, the Palmers donated $2 million to name the Palmer Museum of Art and to expand the building, which was just a simple box structure next to the Creamery while Jack Oswald was president, before they took it on as their major philanthropic commitment. As part of the Palmers' gift, they insisted on bringing a prominent national architect to add a new wing onto the museum. I worked closely with the chair of the physical plant committee of the board to get a special exception to the rule that only Pennsylvania architects could be used for university projects. The Palmers helped select Charles Moore, a leader in American postmodernism, to design the addition. It was one of Moore's last commissions before he died in 1993.

Along with the Palmer Museum, the Arts Festival served as a catalyst for a much greater focus on the arts in the entire region, bringing both visual and performing artists to State College, first in the summer and eventually throughout the year. In 1992, the Arts Festival spawned the People's Choice Festival in Boalsburg, on the property of the Pennsylvania Military Museum, allowing more local artists to participate and gain visibility from the larger Arts Festival effort.

Whereas the Arts Festival's mission was to bring major artists to the Centre Region, the People's Choice Festival was designed to include more local artists and craftspeople. Though there were tensions in the early years, today the People's Choice Festival and the Central Pennsylvania Festival complement one another, collaborating to expand the overall impact of arts in our community.

There had always been so many creative people in State College. In the 1960s, the Arts Festival brought these people together and created a shared sense of responsibility to help more people participate in and enjoy art; in the 1990s, there was a palpable expansion of this awareness and community engagement with the arts. In 1994, The Barash Group established the Sy Barash Bright Ideas Fund at the Arts Festival, to foster innovation as the Arts Festival continued to grow. The Bright Ideas Fund was used, for the first time, to bring Italian street painting to the Festival in 2000. When I die, my name will be added to the award.

In 1996, *Town & Gown,* which was still going strong, completed a major two-year project, *State College: Story of the Century,* for the borough of State College. The book was designed as the anchor of the Centennial celebration and the only hardcover book we ever published. We lost a lot of money on the project, but it also brought new exposure to *Town & Gown* and reminded me how much we were valued as a source of local history, personal stories, and community lore. In 1996 *Town & Gown* also launched my monthly column, "Lunch With Mimi," my favorite, most authentic, and most-enduring work of journalism.

In 1999, Sam and I pledged $1 million to Penn State. I was to pay sixty-seven percent and Sam thirty-three percent. While the pledge was a reminder of all the history we had in common through Penn State, the unequal split was an early sign of financial differences between us that would lead to trouble in the ensuing years.

All this happened while my business experienced its greatest, steadiest years of growth and expansion, owing to my own relentless work ethic and Nan's joining the business and bringing much needed fiscal discipline to our operations. We reorganized the billboard business (Morgan Signs) and the agency (Barash Advertising) as Morgan Signs Inc., doing business as "The Barash Group." Over time we spun off the magazines as Barash Publications (later Barash Media) and Nan started her own division, Barash Group Philadelphia.

My big takeaway from the 1990s was to stick to what I was really good at, to trust my instincts, and to surround myself with people I could trust. My biggest failure was ignoring the rifts that were deepening on key fronts: between me and Sam, between me and Carol, and between Carol and Nan. These would come back to bite me.

It was also in the 1990s, after facing down a second cancer threat in 1993, that I began to seriously focus on writing this book, completing the first draft with the help of local writer Walt Mills

('66). I would talk into a recorder, and then we would sit together and go deeper. He wrote the first draft of that book. As we got a rhythm, and the draft unfolded, he would give me questions to answer into my recorder while driving back and forth to Rye Brook to spend time with Sam.

It would be more than twenty years before Carol and I sat down, over a year of shared storytelling, sorting out the tangled threads between us and enabling me to complete my story for the world.

CHAPTER 30
THE COMPLEXITIES OF MARRIAGE: MY LIFE WITH SAM FREDMAN

Just about the time I had finally, significantly healed from the loss of Sy and was totally immersed in the joys of life, work, and a second loving marriage, I was brought to the edge of a new kind of awakening in 1989. The loss of Lou, with no warning; breast cancer; and facing my first major business failure in The Towers, the bold, visionary project that was emotionally tied to both my first and second husbands, took me to a place I had never experienced before.

Wherever I went, whatever I looked like on the outside, I was surrounded by a palpable, almost physical presence of fear and inadequacy. I felt embarrassed, lonely, helpless, and without the capacity to demonstrate strength. I had lost my ability to rise above disaster wherever and whenever it struck, which is what most people thought of when they think of "Mimi" and how I think of myself. For the first time in my life, I felt I wasn't who I wanted to be or who other people expected me to be.

But even at the bottom, I was learning really important lessons that have served me another twenty-eight years: vital, longstanding relationships played a key role in my recovery; my ability to ask for help got me out of where I was stuck; and my deep and abiding sense of gratitude for all that life had thrown at me—and saved me from—got me out of bed and back into the fray each morning. The last of these was new to me.

Lesson #31: Gratitude is a powerful ingredient in a strong, healthy, happy life.

One thing I always felt lucky about was living in State College, right across the street from the university that had played such a crucial role in all stages of my personal and professional development. Nothing makes me happier than a Penn State home football game on a crisp autumn afternoon. Nothing makes me feel more alive and essentially myself than being able to connect State College and Penn State in some new way that honors multiple points of view and opens up opportunities for people, like myself, who started out with few assets other than their will to flourish and succeed.

I felt an odd sense of safety and security in being the kind of public person I had become in the decade and a half since Sy's death. I learned how important my credit was. Both my literal credit score—from all those years of making timely monthly payments on all my loans—and my standing and reputation as a solid public servant and tough but fair businesswoman helped me avoid bankruptcy and the loss of my major assets when my largest investment failed massively.

My belief that my life was meant to be a beacon and lesson for other people, and especially other women, was another huge catalyst that drove me to do whatever it took to avoid my own death and to prevent personal, financial disaster. On the financial side of things, I had grown up. I was someone who had enough money I controlled myself that I was never dependent on other people. As a girl who grew up poor, that was very important to me, a gift I urge other women to give to themselves.

When it was clear that The Towers was failing, but before I had the courage to admit defeat and take action to recover, I returned to a silly habit I began as a child during World War II: saving my coins "for a rainy day." My apartment is filled with piggy banks: one each for nickels, dimes, and quarters. Craziest of all, I keep an antique copper tub that was once used to make apple butter where I drop my pennies whenever I return home from shopping. The copper tub is so heavy now I have no idea how my children will get it out of here after I die.

Lesson #32: Despair and loss open gates to new opportunity. You just have to see them.

***

I don't remember how Sam proposed or how we decided to get married. It all happened very fast, and I was still very much in shock, not really thinking rationally. Though it was something we almost never spoke about, we were saving one another from grief of unfathomable depth and complexity.

From the start, Sam was very colorful, a big talker, someone who embellished stories with details that might not quite be true but made everyone laugh. Life with Sam was fun and fast-paced. We ate and drank a lot. Sam introduced me to Mario Cuomo and his wonderful wife, Matilda, and we went to one of their children's weddings. Sam was politically connected, in the thick of Westchester County politics since the time he was a young man, and that was a playground in which I enjoyed participating. Through Sam, I met many amazing and interesting women, including Congresswoman Nita Lowey; Leslie Harrington Krauss, in development for the arts at SUNY-Purchase; and his dear friend over many years, Dottie Roer.

Sam Fredman's influence made it possible to connect with key people in three areas that were of great interest to me: politics, the arts, and the larger Jewish community. His influence even got me on a bank board in Westchester County, something I never had the opportunity to enjoy in Pennsylvania. I loved all of that, and I deeply enjoyed the sense of extended family life that included Sam's children and grandchildren, Lou's children and grandchildren, and my own. Passover and Thanksgiving were big gatherings like the ones I remembered from my childhood, and while I was not in love with Sam in the way I had been with Lou or Sy, I experienced it as a good relationship for that time of my life.

All four of the Fredman children, Sam's two sons and their wives, treated me as special, not only as someone who had rescued their father but as someone they liked and respected in my own right. When Lou's son, Sam Coppersmith, was running for the House of Representatives in 1992, I took Sam Fredman's grandson Danny to Phoenix to help with his campaign. That same trip, I taught Danny how to play poker. And I took him to the mall and let him pick out whatever he wanted. That trip was a real high spot for me, connecting the children and grandchildren of my second and third husbands.

Back in White Plains, I baked cookies with Danny's younger sister, Ariele. Even though I'd never baked before, or since, and the cookies were horrible, we had such a wonderful time. I don't remember specific times with Sam's other two grandchildren, who were still quite young, but I have fond memories of them all.

In Rye Brook, I was just a little over an hour from Carol and Jed in New Jersey. This allowed me to take Carol's son Zach to Yankees games and to take her daughters Talia and Eliana shopping and out to eat in New York. Once, I got to sit right behind home plate in a celebrity box at Yankee Stadium because Sam's son, Andy, was doing an architectural project for the Yankees. That was pure pleasure for me. I loved the excitement, the great view, great food, and being with famous people. I got a huge rush having nothing to worry about except the Yankees winning. And when I was in that magical world, I did not think very far beyond its borders.

Part of what attracted me to Sam was his involvement and leadership in a more organized and more substantive Jewish community than was available in State College. We went regularly to Temple Israel, a conservative, egalitarian synagogue in White Plains. Their rabbi, Gordon Tucker, asked big unanswerable questions, reminding me of the probing intellectuals who had led Temple Israel in Wilkes-Barre when I was a child. Tucker had been married to Hadassah Freilich, who later married U.S. Senator Joseph Lieberman, and Sam had been involved in that divorce, so he knew them all quite well. Honestly, I loved being in the thick of all that with him. He knew so many interesting people (and gossip) because of his civic activity as well as his decades of work as a divorce attorney.

In addition to Penn State, there were many important things Sam and I had in common. We were both from modest beginnings with strong mothers and fathers who were extremely ill and physically incapacitated. We were both from Northeast Pennsylvania, and our faith was an important part of our daily life as children. Just as Sy and I had trouble getting our business off the ground, Sam had struggled as a young divorce attorney in New York, in the years when it was hard for Jewish lawyers to get serious business. But living in Westchester, Sam was now part of a large, multi-faceted Jewish community, and Jewish rituals were part of his everyday life.

Sy had little interest in Judaism until very close to his death. Lou was interested in Judaism, but more as an intellectual than as a spiritual concern. Sam was the most actively and joyfully Jewish, so in that sense, it was like coming home to something that I'd drifted away from for most of my adult life.

It was a good enough relationship until it wasn't. Seventeen years, three cars, two serious car accidents, and almost a thousand trips later, the good things stopped being good, and the gunk that had always been just below the surface became toxic. But for all of the 1990s and the early years of the 2000s, I was my own person in State College during the week and quite happy to be Mrs. Sam Fredman on the weekends.

CHAPTER 31
WHEN THE SKY REALLY IS FALLING: THE TOWERS

From the moment in 1966, when Sy and I bought 403 South Allen Street for our office and painted the door trim red, we had dreamed of buying up all the properties on that block, tearing them down, and building a larger structure that included offices, apartments, and public space. We thought it was a perfect location to walk downtown and to campus, and one by one, we bought up all the buildings on our block. Sy and I bought three of the buildings, and I bought the last one, in the late '70s, by myself.

In 1986, at the height of a downtown real estate development boom, Lou and I saw other people making money, and it looked so easy! We decided to take the leap. Our feasibility study pointed out potential drawbacks—the price structure for the forty residential units was too high ($135,000 was the recommended price versus the $160,000 required to make a solid profit)—but we ignored them. State College Federal Savings and Loan was initially very interested in being a partner in our project and then backed out, but we ignored that warning as well.

We broke ground in August 1987, and when Lou died in January, 1989, The Towers was complete and we were preparing to move into our new condominium. We had picked out the furniture together and really splurged. I moved in by myself in February, and in April dedicated the building to my two deceased husbands.

Financially, The Towers was a project that was neither easy nor successful. On the surface, I was doing my best to look like I was holding everything together. But inside, I was a wreck. I turned to the smartest business people I knew for advice, but I wasn't really ready to listen—or deal with the really hard questions.

Phil Sieg, whom I'd first met when Sy was sick in the summer of 1963, came to my office unannounced. He walked in, sat down, and said, "Mimi, stop paying the bank. You have troubled real estate, and it's not going to get better. It's beautiful, but it's ahead of its time. The only one making money is the bank, and you don't want to continue losing money. You have to do a workout with the bank."

Phil was tough, and he wanted me to be tough. He was trying to save me from bankruptcy.

"You've never borrowed money for real estate development before," he went on. "I'm telling you, you've got to stop paying the bank, or you'll lose everything you have." To respond to Phil's genuine concern, I had to pull out all the energy and creativity I had to make myself work.

It took me a full year to get up the courage to take action.

I set a meeting with my bank officer and said, "I just can't keep doing this. The units are selling for less and less, and I can't sell them fast enough to pay the monthly interest, let alone the principal."

Jack Infield ('73) at the bank said, "Give me one more month." I was running out of cash and had started to sell my other real estate to make payments.

When I finally explained my predicament to Sam, he said, "I have a colleague who's a workout lawyer; he'll knock these Central Pennsylvania people out of their chairs. And it won't cost you much money. He'll do it for me."

Sam's colleague, Asher Fensterheim, looked and acted just like the name sounded. I paid to have a driver bring him to State College and met him for the first time half an hour before we were going into the bank conference room for the workout.

He came to my office, picked me up, and said, "Just follow everything I do. Follow my instructions." He gave me an outline. "All you have to know is whatever I ask you to do, follow me."

I had no idea what a workout was. Up until that point, I always paid all my principal and interest on time. Everything, from mortgages to multiple business loans and Carol's Yale tuition, I paid on time monthly.

We met at the bank's business office, upstairs on South Atherton Street. We walked into the big conference room, and everyone else was already there. The lawyer representing Lou's estate, a woman, was at the head of the table. Lou had co-signed the loan, so it was as if he was there at all the meetings.

Before we walked in, Asher reminded me, "follow my lead," and sat across the table from me so I could watch his moves.

Chuck Pearson, president of the bank, opened the meeting, stating the goal and introducing the participants, and then he excused himself. The bank's workout lawyer, from Pittsburgh and sitting to my left, started to chit chat.

"Coppersmith, I know that name..."

"That guy is my late husband," I said, "he would be so disappointed that I hit rocky road without him."

Lou's estate attorney looked at me gently. It might have been my optimism playing tricks, but I really felt like she was reassuring me that it wasn't going to be as bad as I thought. It felt wonderful just to have another woman in the room who wasn't there to take notes.

Lesson #33: Look for camaraderie. If you pay attention, you'll see others in the same boat as you.

The bank's local attorney got on his high horse: "We've got to have at least eight percent interest."

I knew there was no way I could pay that. They were proposing to take over the twenty-five remaining units and sell them, along with the parking spaces—their idea was to secure the workout by using the twenty-eight extra parking spaces as collateral. I had some revenue from leased commercial space I had rented to Penn State and some other tenants, but during the year I was afraid to take action, I had already sold some of the commercial space. So I had very few options. Putting such a high interest on the shortfall—$2,450,000—felt almost as bad as credit card debt.

The lawyers were talking to one another, as if I wasn't even there. Their voices got a bit louder; their demands hardened. All of a sudden Asher slammed his briefcase shut.

"Mimi, I thought we were here to work this out, but we're not. Let's go." I had spent my entire life focused on talking and building relationships. I had to go against all my instincts to look down and follow him briskly out of the room. "Don't worry," Asher assured me. "They'll be back in thirty to forty-five minutes with an offer."

Jack Infield came out twenty-eight minutes later.

"Please come back in," he said.

The interest rate was five percent; payments wouldn't start for a month or two, so we had time to regroup; and the Coppersmith Estate would be charged $500,000. I paid between $12,000 to $14,000 a month until I made the last payment on November 3, 2014—honestly, one of the happiest days of my business life.

Lou and I had never talked about what we'd do if our idea didn't work. My only goal for The Towers was to end up with a mortgage-free office space and additional income from renting office space to others. I hadn't realized how tough it was to sell high-end residential space in downtown State College, which had become crowded and noisy from an excess of student housing and bars. The influx of retirees returning to State College was still a decade in the future.

This was the largest financial mistake I ever made, and the most emotionally painful slice of business because the project was tied to not one, but two men I dearly loved. I felt like I had let them both down. But all of that emotional weight is also why it took me so long to make a sound business move and to do something that I had never done before. The Towers is successful now, and I am paying the $500,000 back to Lou's estate, so his children do not suffer for my mistake.

Looking back, I see how very cocky I was my entire life in business. I was a woman with no business training, not even an accounting course in college. I was a public person, a teacher, an advocate for those who were less well off. But when I was confused about business, there were a few very successful local men—Jack Wilkinson, his brother Roy ('36), and Phil Sieg—who gave me great advice. Bill Schreyer, with whom I served on the Penn State Board of Trustees, became another trusted friend and business ally.

Lesson #34: Stick to what you know, and do your best; listen to the advice of experts, but also trust your instincts.

There was one horrible meeting where the architect demeaned and bullied me as a woman. I called a meeting with Lou, our attorney, and the architect's attorney to cancel our contract because the architect had been abusive to me on several occasions. The attorneys—my attorney wink-winking with the architect's attorney and with Lou—talked me out of cancelling the contract. The architect promised to behave more professionally, but in reality, he never did

To this day, I wish I hadn't let myself be overruled by the men in the room, including Lou, because it made things so much harder to negotiate once Lou was gone. In 1994, I took the abusive architect to mediation and won a $450,000 judgement against his farm in Bellefonte. But it was a pyrrhic victory: after years of negotiating, in the end we were paid only $10,000.

Lesson #35: When the sky is falling and you're not sure what to do, you need to engage others you can trust. To rely on your own indecision is dangerous.

Most people I know and respect are happy to help others be successful and avoid mistakes. That's what we're here for! We want future generations to learn from our mistakes, not repeat them. My granddaughters don't really understand this about me: that I was the lone female wolf making my way against great odds, and that the people I most often had to turn to were men. That's just how it was then, and I hope how it will never be for their generation.

CHAPTER 32
IF NOT NOW, WHEN? CELEBRATING MY SIXTIETH BIRTHDAY WITH MY DAUGHTERS

When Carol and Nan asked me what I wanted for my sixtieth birthday in 1993, after a short pause I said, "To have a bat mitzvah with both of you!" Since I had shown almost no interest in religion when they were young, I think they were both quite surprised.

Lesson #36: One of the things my parents taught me was to *ask* for what you want. "You'll never know unless you ask," my mother used to say, and it's true—in sales and all of life.

Being Jewish had always been important to me, a source of confidence, persistence, and the will to endure. I attended Hebrew School at Temple Israel and experienced leadership there for the first time, but I never had the opportunity for a bat mitzvah because Conservative synagogues like Temple Israel did not yet include women in that Jewish rite of passage from childhood to adulthood.

When the time came for my girls to go to Hebrew School, some girls in State College and young women at Penn State were beginning to participate equally in Jewish worship. But my daughters had no interest, and I did not insist. I regretted that they did not have the strong, traditional Jewish education that nurtured me as a child, but Sy and I were very assimilated. We gave our daughters dance lessons, skating lessons, and sports camps, rather than any sustained Jewish activity.

As women came to take their equal role beside men in Judaism, I developed a secret desire to become an adult in the Jewish community, through a bat mitzvah service. I thought it would be a great experience to do this together with the girls—who were now thirty-five and thirty-two, with children of their own. Of course, there were some major hurdles to overcome. Carol and Nan were both pregnant. We lived in three different communities, and each of us needed a tutor. After protracted discussions, we agreed to celebrate our b'nei mitzvah at Carol and her husband Jed's synagogue, Congregation Oheb Shalom in South Orange, New Jersey.

Each of us received a set of tapes to help us memorize the Torah service, and we prepped on our own, pulling together the last details for the bat mitzvah in person just the day before. It was not so hard for me, as I still remembered the words and rhythms from attending Saturday services and Hebrew School three days a week as a child. But all of this was relatively new for the girls and solid work. I was so grateful that they put in the time so we could share this ritual together.

The day of the b'nei mitzvah was very moving for me; people came from far and wide to share the celebration with us, and it felt like a real personal triumph. There are so many times when I fear I've faltered in bringing my daughters—and their husbands and children—together for important life events. While I get along well with both my daughters, and I now feel very close to each of them, over the years they have drifted apart. We've had many moments when hope is in sight, but then it slips away again. Standing together by the Torah, receiving shared blessings from the rabbi, our b'nei mitzvah was one of those transcendent moments when we were all together for something larger and more enduring than our individual needs. I hope with everything I have that my daughters figure out how to do that more often, if not in my lifetime, then in theirs.

CHAPTER 33
THE POWER OF EVERYDAY CONVERSATIONS: LUNCH WITH MIMI

One of the most important features of today's *Town & Gown* was a radically new idea when it was brought to me in 1995, by Mike Poorman ('82), our manager of publications. He was studying national trends, looking for ways to connect more powerfully with our readership and to establish reliable, replicable content with a unique personal touch. This was years before social media took off, but the idea was part of the same drive for authenticity and connection that is behind so much of what works on the internet today.

Mike suggested that for the January 1996 thirtieth-anniversary issue we launch "Lunch With Mimi," a series of casual conversations, over lunch, with people who had shaped—and were continuing to inform—the community. He had a list of people to interview, starting with Arnold Addison, Mayor of State College, and head football coach, Joe Paterno.

Over the years, "Lunch with Mimi" has allowed me to interview more than 250 kind and talented individuals who influenced the present and future of State College and Penn State. Preparing to complete this book, I interviewed another forty-eight people, using the same casual, kitchen table format that made "Lunch with Mimi" so fulfilling for me and so beloved by our readers over the years.

I am grateful for this long run of monthly conversations. They return me, once every month, to my early training as a student journalist, and they keep me in touch with the new, groundbreaking things that are taking root all around us. These innovators encourage and enable us to expand the ways we think and act in this small, still quite conservative college town. These monthly conversations help to keep me in the present and future. They give me hope on days when I might otherwise turn inward or backward and feel glum.

"Lunch with Mimi" has become a key component of my public persona. It has been a great success for me personally and for the magazine. Readers tell us what they like, and it's often quite surprising: a woman minister, a local artist, an unsung hero who works mostly behind the scenes. In fact, it's not the superstars, but the everyday citizens that most interest our readers. These interviews are one of the things I most enjoy doing, and really prepare for, because they help me contribute to a better-informed community.

This might seem like a very local lesson, and there's a sense in which it is.

Lesson #37: Each of us, to be successful, needs to establish and maintain a voice and presence in public.

Women, even otherwise confident women, are often reluctant to put themselves forward in this way. "Lunch with Mimi" is a very female framework: just talking to people over lunch. That is both its delight and its power, and what has made it such an extraordinary platform for dialogue and change in our community.

Looking back to my failed attempt to use *Town & Gown* as my political platform in the late 1960s, I see how much more influence I've had over the years, by including a much wider range of people in my world, asking them great questions, and letting them and their ideas take center stage.

CHAPTER 34
FAILURE IS PART OF THE FUN: FUNDRAISING FABLES

As I reflect on how I rebuilt my sense of joy and purpose in the 1990s, fundraising for causes I'm passionate about was a key component of that renewal. Fundraising, which is really just sales for nonprofits, required that I face my fear of failure again and again.

Lesson #38: Helping others can help you get past where you might be stuck emotionally.

I remember many laughable moments, and a few sad ones, in that process.

Going back to the 1980s, when I was still a novice at fundraising, I recall a meeting with W. K "Bill" Ulerich ('31) at his cozy second-floor office in Clearfield—complete with a kitchen and an executive assistant at his beck and call. Bill, a self-made millionaire, graduated with a B.A. in Journalism from Penn State. He worked for the *Centre Daily Times* and was among the founders of WMAJ, the first radio station in State College. The tower for that radio station was the first time anyone other than the university was allowed to build on university land.

I was helping my dear friend, Barb Palmer, raise $2 million for the Hemlock Girl Scout Council, serving seven counties in Central Pennsylvania. At that time, I felt that I would not be taken seriously if I made the ask alone. To help solicit Ulerich, I enlisted Alan Walker, CEO of Bigler Coal, another leading businessman in Clearfield County.

Alan and I arrived at Ulerich's office and got the conversation going. In the midst of chit chat about Ulerich's various businesses, Bill pulled an index card from his inside jacket pocket.

"I am proud to say," he began, "my cash position is strong. I check it every morning and keep it right here." And with that he put the card away.

I had what I needed.

"Thank you for sharing your success, in so many visible ways, in the local community," I began. "You've been a real stalwart supporter of the Boy Scouts, and I'd like you to consider a similar gift to the Girl Scouts, as part of their first-ever capital campaign." And then I waited what seemed like forever for his response.

"Tell me how much Kurtz (Kurtz Bros Office Supplies) gave," he asked, his face showing no emotion.

"Fifteen," I responded.

"Well I always like to beat them, so I'll give you $20,000." Those of us experienced at sales know that once you've got it, close it and move on. Alan and I did just that! After we completed the paperwork for Bill's signature, we headed down the stairs to the street, and began giggling together. Kurtz had given $1,500! My answer of "fifteen" was completely innocent; I was just following Bill's lead and answering his questions as directly as I could. He let us know his cash position was strong; he shared that his philanthropy was partly a competition for local acclaim; and he was completely in charge the whole time. That's how fundraising often works when you do your homework: ask thoughtful questions and let the other person take the lead in the conversation.

For that same campaign, one of my first calls—all by myself—targeted my friends, Barb and Jim Palmer. Barb had taken me to lunch and used our friendship to get me involved in this campaign, and now it was my turn to call on them.

I decided to take them to dinner at Joey Z's. I needed to get a few five and six-figure gifts early in order to ensure a successful campaign. Cliff Jones ('72), my Campaign Co-Chair, and I carefully targeted the best prospects. His were mostly people who ran large corporations in the greater Harrisburg area, and mine were in the smaller, surrounding counties.

Jim responded very quickly with an offer of $77,000. Jim was well known for his generous record of support of both the Boy Scouts and Girl Scouts over the last decade, and I had anticipated a much larger gift. He indicated quite strongly that this was their best offer.

"Please give it some more thought," I said quietly. "I was

161

expecting more. For this campaign to succeed, for me to get this done, we need six-figure lead gifts. I'd like you to take some more time and think about it." We finished our dinner, enjoyed dessert, and went home.

For some time, there was utter silence on the topic. No further conversation evolved, even over a short winter vacation Lou and I took with them to their winter home on Grand Cayman.

On April 1, 1987, Barb appeared in my office unannounced. I invited her into our conference room, and she reported that she and Jim had finally decided on their gift. She held out the pledge card, and it said "$25,000."

After a short pause, and a stop of my heartbeat, she removed her thumb from the corner of the pledge card and said, "April Fools," revealing the largest gift of the campaign--$250,000.

***

By the spring of 1996, when Associate Athletic Director Ellen Perry ('69), head of women's athletics, convened a group of women leaders to consider the challenge of getting more television time for women's intercollegiate athletics, particularly for the Lady Lions basketball team, I was deeply involved in local philanthropy. There were no funds at the university to support this, though the team was gaining in prominence in the Big 10 and nationally.

Thinking of Emily's List, the political action committee (PAC) that provides early support to left-leaning women candidates ("Early Money Is Like Yeast"), I suggested, "Why couldn't Penn State Athletics have Rene's list?" building off the reputation of Rene Portland, who had been the coach of women's basketball for more than a decade.

Off we went, dribbling, passing, shooting for the big shots. Very quickly we had raised enough not only to broadcast some of the bigger games on TV, but also to launch a weekly program about Lady Lions Basketball, "Centre Court With Rene Portland."

We consciously targeted prominent women, small businesses that appealed to women, and corporations that would be expected to join women's efforts towards equality. We raised over $100,000 from 150 contributors in the first year and had a strong second year, enabling us to televise four women's basketball games, as well as one women's gymnastics meet and one women's volleyball match.

Then, we hit a roadblock. We were told by those in charge at the university to cease and desist our fundraising efforts. Our efforts didn't conform to the university's fundraising guidelines, they insisted, and it was unfair to other coaches. Rene was later accused of discrimination against lesbian players, and she was forced to leave Penn State. Penn State settled the case. But I still have my Rene's List lapel pin that I wore with special pride. And the idea to support Lady Lion basketball with television programming continues through Coquese Washington and her weekly show, "Courtside with Coquese."

Lesson #39: Be as direct as humanly possible. It's difficult to determine how far you can go if you don't push occasionally.

For me, this meant it was definitely worth a stretch ask with a serious prospect. You want to make them feel important; you want to state the nonprofit's need without overstating it; and you want to speak to the donor's power and ability to influence the organization without too much flattery.

Philanthropy, even on a small scale, enables people to experience the power and potential of their generosity. My philanthropic work has brought me many of the greatest joys and deepest friendships of my eighty-five years of life.

CHAPTER 35
MY DAUGHTERS AND MY BUSINESS: A DANGEROUS MIX

When Lou was at the Cleveland Clinic for his angioplasty in 1986, Nan flew out to meet us. She was living in Philadelphia, selling advertising for Channel 17, WPHL, an independent television station.

One of Nan's key clients at the station, Charles Genuardi, Vice President of Genuardi's Family Markets, had taken her to lunch to ask her if she would leave the station and buy his media moving forward. He said he was soon going to assume leadership of his family's business and planned to grow the chain of upscale supermarkets into a billion-dollar company.

"What did he say next?" Lou looked up from his hospital bed.

Nan described Charles Genuardi turning over his menu and saying, "You can do what your mother does in State College, but do it in Philly and Genuardi's will be your first client. I will pay you $15,000 for your work in the first year." I told Nan it was a crazy idea and she should stick with her secure job in television.

Lou kept going and told her, "Go back to the hotel and figure out what it would take for you to live for a year." When she came back the next day and said $25,000, Lou said if she could get $30,000 from Genuardi, he'd convince me that it was a good idea.

When Nan went back to Charles Genuardi with her counter offer, he agreed to it, and we worked up plans to employ her at The Barash Group. She ran the Philadelphia office out of her home, with part-time help from our staff.

From the beginning, Nan was very much running her own territory. I felt she also made me a better businesswoman in many ways. For example, I used to let people owe us money forever; it was hard for me to push people who had overextended themselves. Our accounts receivable were aging, and we did not have a plan or process to address that. Nan helped us tackle this head on. She would not tolerate slow-paying customers; she simply let those relationships go.

Nan brought tremendous creativity to our promotional products business, establishing a separate business unit called Barash Promotions. We had previously treated promotional products—pens, buttons, stadium blankets, you name it--as add-ons to our agency business. Using promotional products to open new doors, Nan was able to build a portfolio of significant agency business in Philadelphia, and with her intense focus on promotions, she was able to identify new, larger opportunities with all of our agency clients.

Nan had the courage and desire to bring bigger customers into our portfolio, showing us we had the capacity to break through and service them. Nan's early work as the rookie sales person entertaining clients at sporting events for Channel 17 gave her the chance to meet people in charge of marketing at large corporations. Some of her early clients included Bell of Pennsylvania, Pep Boys, and Astra Zeneca. Nan earned the opportunity to compete for national business, tenaciously won it, and then expanded it steadily for two decades. Like Central Counties Bank in the 1970s, Nan's Philadelphia-based customers often challenged us and pushed us in exciting new directions.

Nan also had the good fortune of beginning her journey at The Barash Group with an established, very well-known and respected business name in Philadelphia as her anchor client. So when she opened doors to new prospects she could say we did business for Genuardi's.

Charles Genuardi was the second generation to run the family business, but there was no one in the third generation of cousins to take over after him. One of the last big jobs we did for Genuardi's was a book all about the history and growth of the company. Nan never asked why we were creating the book. After the final proof was approved, she was told by Genuardi that his team would drop in the financials directly with the printer. He added that they only needed twenty-five copies of a creative project that cost over $25,000 to produce. When Nan relayed this story to her accountant husband that night, he told her, "Nan, they are for sale."

Nan's joining The Barash Group was a gift to me. Nan brought fresh, young ideas, and energy and helped me to think bigger. Working together, we opened new areas of exploration, and we also paid close attention to the bottom line.

***

After Lou's death, my experience with breast cancer, and the failure of The Towers in the early 1990s, I thought seriously about my own mortality. I didn't want my business failures to be a financial burden on my daughters when I died. I nurtured a hope that Nan would one day take over leadership of our family business when I retired, but rarely spoke to her about it. When I did bring it up, she said she had no interest.

At that point, the business was highly leveraged and short of cash, and I was still quite frightened about the prospect of bankruptcy. I had grown up poor, and nothing frightened me more than the fear of losing money and losing control. Those two things—money and control— were both at stake in my vague and largely internal thoughts about what would happen to the business after my death.

Once I had gotten The Towers under better control through the workout with the bank, I began talking to my lawyer, accountant, and insurance broker about three interconnected issues: how to keep the business running, take care of the huge liability on The Towers, and protect my daughters from financial exposure when I died. I spoke with my advisors and came up with a plan to give my shares of Morgan Signs to Nan, to give some other stock to Carol, and to set up an irrevocable trust for insurance on my life owned by the business. All of this required Carol's as well as Nan's signatures.

Without any discussion, I sent the paperwork to Carol to sign. She was devastated that I had not talked to her first. She felt that Nan was receiving—both monetarily and emotionally—a much larger share than she was being given. At the time, Carol and I had no framework to sort through the many layers of painful history unleashed by this situation. We said many unkind things to one another, which I believe we would both take back now if we could. The thing she said that hurt me most was, "I don't need you to be my banker. I need you to be my mother."

I felt physically assaulted at the time she said that, and to this day, I experience a creeping pain under my skin when I think back on that conversation. Those words haunted me for years and prevented me from seeing all the ways Carol was trying to close the gap between us. The broken ways she and I saw one another and communicated with one another for the next two decades flowed from that rupture—and the way it repeated my fear and emotional rejection of Carol after Sy died.

Lesson #40: Do not avoid difficult conversations with those you love most. When things are most complicated, and differences of opinion most likely, it is important—as the mother or the CEO (and especially when you are both)—to be the person who has the courage to lead those difficult, but essential, conversations.

***

Three years later in 1996, the Princeton-Rutgers Center for Electronic Texts in the Humanities, an early EdTech think tank where Carol was the Associate Director, lost its director, and Carol was exploring what to do next professionally. Nan suggested that we invite her to join The Barash Group.

Carol asked, bluntly, "Is there a place for me at the table or has Nan already taken it?"

I responded, "Let's see how it goes, and if you like it, we'll figure out how to find you a long-term role."

I was naive and hopeful that somehow everything would work out without my active intervention.

Unlike Nan, who showed up at The Barash Group with a piece of business that covered her salary and provided an anchor for her, Carol arrived with significant online experience but nothing directly related to our traditional advertising business. However, right out of the gate she was very good at sales. She networked aggressively and brought in important new client relationships: Jaguar Cars, Princeton University, and Saint Barnabas Health Care.

She understood how to nurture those relationships and grow them from a small initial sale to something much larger. There were several opportunities where her client relationships enabled us to work together: the NFL push to connect with women through the

167

Susan G. Komen Race for the Cure; the opening of Princeton University Stadium in 1998; and a campaign to rebrand *Seventeen* magazine that included print media, a DVD, and big posters all over New York City.

Like Nan in Philadelphia, Carol was using her New York base to build an entirely new part of the agency business. Unlike Nan, who almost never crossed me and never did so in public, Carol was quite direct in sharing her ideas about how we could grow and improve the business. Carol's ideas, as well as her approach, tended to threaten me, reopening the rift between us.

While Nan was drawn to the nuts and bolts of the business, things like how to increase profitability by improving collections, Carol was most interested in how we could expand our business through online products and services. This was the work she was doing before she came to The Barash Group, and she could see—long before most people—where it was going. I was a bit afraid of all that change and urged her to be patient and stick with our core business.

Carol came to State College once a month for our sales and leadership team meetings, staying overnight at my apartment, and it was during this time that we really got to know one another for the first time. I enjoyed the time Carol and I spent together and could sense that she was genuinely interested in me and my ideas. My relationship with Carol, which could be tense but also showed signs of improvement, was complicated by the fact that both Sam and Nan had their own issues with Carol.

Carol was direct to a fault, and this often made me feel quite out of control. I remember one family dinner early on in my life in White Plains: we were all seated around a beautiful table, with fancy china and a nice dinner we had all prepared together. I can't remember what we were talking about, but Sam was at the head of the table going on and on, having had perhaps one too many drinks. He made a rhetorical flourish, "I really wonder what you all think about that," and then kept talking.

Carol interrupted him, "Well if you'd pause to listen for a second, maybe the rest of us could speak."

Shocked looks and a couple snickers went around the table. I suspect most of us thought something similar, but no one dared to cross Sam. He was physically large and dominated many conversations. It was something the rest of us took for granted. Carol never apologized, and Sam never forgave her. Between that antagonism and the fact that Nan and I were working closely together in the business, I saw Carol and her family very little in the 1990s, before we began working together.

By the fall of 1998, when Carol was bringing in six-figure opportunities to The Barash Group from her New York area clients, she broached the idea of me promoting her from a sales role to one that included both sales and leadership of an internet division. That's when things started to unravel. She had a very clear idea of how she could add value by moving the business in a new direction. As she became more insistent, I felt increasingly threatened and started to avoid the discussion altogether. In my own mind I was saying "no," but out loud to Carol I kept saying, "I need more time to think about it."

In September, in front of the other senior managers at our annual planning meeting, Carol asked, "When are we going to talk about the internet side of the business? Is it or isn't it part of your long-term planning?"

I am not at all proud of what happened next. I pushed my chair back from the table and said, "Obviously there's not enough room here for both of us, so I am going to leave." And I walked out to catch my breath and regain my cool.

Maybe fifteen minutes later, I returned, and we finished the meeting.

Afterward, Carol and I drove to my office. I sat behind my desk, and she sat across from me.

"Mom," she said, "I'm going to make this easy for you. I don't want to threaten you, and I don't want to make you feel the way you feel right now. I need some time to figure out what I'm going to do next, but I will leave The Barash Group by the end of the year."

***

Because I felt so overwhelmed by the whole situation and knew many things needed clarification, but couldn't begin to talk about them, I turned to my attorney for advice. In October, I called Carol and Nan to my attorney's office in Philadelphia, and my attorney told Carol that, in his opinion, it was not in the best fiduciary interest of the business for her to remain involved. I told her she could take her clients and do whatever she wanted with them, since she had built those relationships.

"You didn't need to call in a lawyer, mom," she said in tears, as she left the room alone, her head hung low. "I get that you don't want me as part of the family business. I told you I would leave by the end of the year."

***

When Carol officially opened her new online marketing business in December, I wrote a formal letter to all of her customers and all of our suppliers, saying I had nothing to do with her new company, exactly what I would have done if another employee had left to start a separate business. A few weeks later, Carol returned her company car and computer, and drove off. We were both deeply wounded by the whole experience, but we never talked about the personal side of our ruptured business relationship.

Though I never said this directly to her, I was—and still am—quite overwhelmed and intimidated by technology. I didn't feel the business could make that leap and still be safe. I was afraid, both financially and intellectually, of the direction Carol recommended, and I wanted to stick to what I knew best. I really didn't open my mind to her ideas at any point.

But why did I feel so threatened, not just by what she was proposing, but by Carol herself? And why did I give her such mixed signals throughout her time at The Barash Group, on the one hand encouraging her to think of herself as a potential leader but unwilling to let her lead in any significant way?

I think this really goes back to something very deep in my makeup about needing to be in control. My first two husbands understood this about me and gave me plenty of room to be myself. Sam Fredman didn't get this, and we often fought or avoided one another so that we wouldn't fight. Nan gave me the space I needed to run the show, while providing her input in a clearly supporting role. Carol was asking that I work more directly with her, and that I be more honest—with myself and with her—than I was able to be at the time.

This is long before I faced my own demons, and at that time I was very afraid of both my daughters. I felt I had let them down when they were younger and very rarely told them what I expected. And then when they disappointed me, I was like a wounded animal, mute and helpless. Nan could sense this behavior coming and learned to avoid it and work around it. And when she saw Carol causing me this kind of pain, she leapt to my rescue, rather than leaving us to work things through.

It was impossible to explore giving Carol some part of The Barash Group, or creating a new part of the business which she would manage, without discussing it with Nan because she now owned nearly half of the company shares of the company. I had kept the only voting share of the company, so I could have created a solution if I'd wanted to. Because I had worked so closely with Nan for so many years, I felt I needed to talk to Nan about it. But for some reason I could not. I'm not sure exactly why I avoided that discussion—it's buried so deep I barely remember those years—but avoid it I did.

Looking back, I see how Carol came to the business first and foremost to heal things with me and make peace with me, but that was not yet possible from my side of the table. In the business, I expected people to give me plenty of room and to let me lead. I did not feel that she gave me that space. In the end, I treated her like an ungrateful subordinate, like someone who threatened me and my business.

The 1990s were painful for both of us, and this chapter is the hardest of everything I've tried to share in this book for other women's learning and growth.

1. Barb Palmer and I wearing our bonnets for an outdoor fundraiser.

2. Giving a commencement address at the College of Earth and Mineral Science.

3. Carol Herrmann was my confidant and ally in navigating many challenges and opportunities as a member of the board.

4. Nan and Carol at the Centre Foundation awards dinner where Barb Palmer endowed an award for women leaders in my honor 2017.

5. Homecoming Parade Honorary Marshall 2012.

173

THE 2000s

I don't remember very many specific details from my personal life in the early years of the new century, but things I'd avoided for years came back in overwhelming waves that I could no longer ignore. My resume lists dozens of committees on which I served, projects I chaired, and awards I won. I was driving important breakthroughs in the community by leading major fund-raising initiatives for our local EMS and breast cancer services. On the one hand, my work was valued and I was valued, which gave my life meaning. On the other hand, I was running myself ragged. I was drinking and eating far too much, and I was not really happy.

On September 11, 2001, I was on my way from our home in Rye Brook with my general manager, Dick Hall, and his wife, Nanci, to attend the Outdoor Advertising Association of America Convention at the Hilton in New York. We were also scheduled to have lunch with representatives of the national Easter Seals, who were running a capital campaign to expand their facilities in State College. Just as our country was split apart that day by forces we had not previously recognized as dangerous, my life was breaking open as well.

On the surface, most people had no idea how tenuous my sense of self had become. Most days I ignored it myself. Sam and I had begun making plans for our shared retirement. In 2003, we built and moved into a new home on Honors Lane in The Village at Penn State, near Toftrees.

By the time I turned sixty in 1993, in addition to the renewed sense of spirituality that drove me toward my bat mitzvah with my daughters, I was very focused on activism for women's health and equality. In 2004, I was invited to speak about "Gender Equity - 32 years after Title IX" at a Penn State Forum, and in 2006, I launched the first "Think Pink" Lady Lions Basketball game to benefit breast cancer treatment, access to which had saved my life.

With sponsorship from Kish Bank, "Lunch with Mimi Live" was born in 2005. My greatest joy in this period came from the times I was able to bring together other women—across everyone I knew—to discuss complicated topics that were vital to the community and especially to women. In this live forum, I leaned toward topics that had once frightened me and where, frankly, I felt I had failed: the balance of work and personal life, health and wellness, and even grief. "Lunch with Mimi Live" brought together the journalist, the catalyst, and the community leader in me, and I genuinely loved it.

I was deeply involved in leading the local business community and expanding access to the arts throughout the region. In 2006, the State College Business Privilege tax was repealed. This tax had been bleeding local small businesses, and I was an outspoken voice to get it repealed. I invested in the Broadway production of *The Producers* an sponsored the touring version at Penn State's Center for the Performing Arts.

All thirteen of my grandchildren graduated from high school and went to college in the 2000s. Several graduated from college and started their first jobs. All this time, I was driving most weekends and some weeks to Rye Brook to be with Sam. When I arrived, his former secretary, Carolyn, was often there, or I could smell the hint of her perfume and knew she'd been there recently. Occasionally I wondered if there was something I should worry about, and every now and again, I'd ask Sam about it.

But he said, "Mimi, don't be silly. She's an old family friend. It's nothing." And then in the fall of 2007, while I was contemplating different options for selling my business, I could no longer ignore the facts of my husband's infidelity.

I was angry and embarrassed; I lacked the energy to get out of bed and go to the office. The old demons of shame and failure, which I'd experienced since I was a little girl, haunted my waking as well as my sleep. In a matter of days, my marriage and my life started to collapse. In the process of selling my business and confronting Sam's infidelity, at once, I fell into an overwhelming depression. It was impossible to hide the obvious symptoms: I had no hunger, no energy, no zest for life. Several times, Carol or Nan came to my rescue, driving to State College to help me get out of bed, get dressed, and get out of the house. After years and years of drinking, I finally gave it up completely to help claw myself out of depression.

In February 2008, I sold Morgan Signs, and then I sold Barash Publications in June, since Nan had no interest in running those parts of the business. Those deals brought in more money than I'd ever dreamed of. It was a real bonus to remain a consultant to *Town & Gown*, which was really like a third child to me. That year *Town & Gown* received the Arnold Addison Award from the State College Borough Council for our positive role recording the history of the borough.

The process of divorce stretched from 2008 to 2010. I purchased a condominium just one floor below my dear friend Barb Palmer. Living close to Barb helped immeasurably with my overall recovery during those hard-fought years, battling back from depression and onto my own two feet emotionally, really, for the first time. And during those years, as I eased out of the crazy pace of running my own business and back into the things I love most, I rediscovered the joys of so many women friends, including, at long last, my daughter Carol, who is sitting here with me and helping me share my story with others.

CHAPTER 36
SEE THE BIG PICTURE: FROM ALPHA AMBULANCE TO CENTRE LIFELINK EMS

Early in 2001, Scott Rawson ('86), executive director of Alpha Community Ambulance, invited me to a small meeting in one of the dark upstairs rooms at the historic Hotel State College. Dan Nestlerode ('66), the treasurer, and John Spearly ('77), president, were also in the room. Together, they walked me through a presentation that explained the urgent need for a new ambulance headquarters in town as well as a satellite station on University Drive at the south end of the borough. The area's rapid growth and the preponderance of students needing emergency medical care screamed for the acquisition of more modern, sophisticated equipment to meet escalating emergency situations.

Based on my experience as a member of the Penn State board and my growing reputation as a volunteer fundraiser, Alpha Ambulance leadership sought my advice about how to launch this major building campaign. While this project may not sound sexy, it's the kind of thing that really piqued my interest: leveraging my relationships in town and on campus, my joy in getting big new projects off the ground, and my sense that this was deeply needed in the community.

In 2001, there were only two stand-alone ambulances in our growing community, one owned and operated by the university and one by Centre Community Hospital (now Mt. Nittany Health System). Alpha Ambulance served all other emergencies, since 1941, using an entirely volunteer staff. Over the decades, as demand increased, it became harder and harder for Alpha Ambulance to staff the local EMS service with volunteers. This was another part of the challenge that spoke to my temperament and experience: how to motivate more volunteers, while at the same time recruiting a corps of professional emergency medical staff.

I recall that first meeting with Alpha Ambulance leadership as very focused and no-nonsense. I told them I thought it would be impossible to raise the $1.5 million they needed without professional fundraising staff. They would need a case statement and a team that could recruit and lead prominent local volunteers to pull it all off. They agreed that the challenges were significant. I told them I would begin a conversation with Penn State, without whom the project's success remained doubtful. This discussion needed to take place immediately, I explained, as the university's involvement would define the potential scope of the project. For me, emergency medical services exemplified the kind of program that required the interdependence of town and gown to succeed.

Being aware of the importance of the whole project, and speaking to key stakeholders first, I was able to get that project from an idea to a viable plan in a very short period of time.

Lesson #41: See the big picture and get the right people on board early. With this beginning, great things can happen.

I arranged a meeting with Penn State President Graham Spanier, Scott, Dan, and me. We met in Spanier's office and presented our plan. We requested a lead gift of $250,000 to $500,000 from the university and sought their involvement in encouraging faculty, staff, and administrators to contribute as well.

Graham quickly dismissed the idea.

"As a 501(c)3 nonprofit," he explained, "Penn State does not make any cash contributions to other nonprofits. But, we clearly understand and appreciate the need for a major expansion. Perhaps we can be helpful in other ways. For example, we have lots of land. Where are you thinking of putting the new building?"

We had not yet crossed that bridge. But I sensed an opening and immediately shifted gears to follow Graham's train of thought. With more research, we discovered that the original tower for State College's first radio station, WMAJ, was on university land. This served as a precedent for the university to provide a long-term lease to Alpha Ambulance. The WMAJ tower sat adjacent to an unused site, which we proposed would work well for Alpha's new headquarters. Being so close to the university, the new site would also improve speed of service to the campus in an emergency. Spanier reviewed our proposal with his leadership team, recommended it to the trustees, and got it passed swiftly.

We were off and running. The land at the time was appraised at $300,000. An unusually quick decision led to formalizing a 50-year land lease for $1 per year. It was one of those times when seemingly complicated issues fell into place quite easily.

With the location approved by both sides of College Avenue, we turned to fund-raising. It was much too big a job for me to run as a volunteer. We needed not only serious marketing materials, but a name change to reflect a much bigger mission, as well as the infrastructure to organize and keep track of the entire fundraising effort. I suggested that the Barash Group contribute all the creative materials, as well as the organizational know-how for $150,000, which was five percent of the final campaign goal of $3 million. That was a tiny sum, really, for the amount of work done by my entire team—and I didn't even bill my hours—but it was such a rich and rewarding project to have the opportunity to orchestrate the campaign and make a measurable difference for our community.

Our next challenge was to change the name to reflect the vital role EMS played in the entire combined community, as well as the service's vision and growth trajectory. We came up with the name "LifeLink" to combine a sense of urgency and the life-saving capacity of the expanded service, and the new name really resonated with our volunteers.

It was not easy to put together a high-powered volunteer committee and oversee its smooth and productive function, including regular meetings. To complicate the challenge, the organization's goal posts frequently shifted. The original goal was $1.5 million for the new main facility. In the end we raised over $3 million to fund the new headquarters on Puddletown Road in College Township as well a second site off University Drive, plus additional funds to pay a larger and more extensively trained staff.

We kicked off the fundraising campaign in February 2002 at a grand party at Rider Auto, recognizing Adam Taliaferro ('05) with the first Community Courage Award. Our comprehensive fundraising strategy included participation from the university and local, state, and federal government, as well as a broad community appeal. We arrived at goals for each municipality served by the new facilities, based on their call volume and assigned twenty-five percent of the goal ($750,000) to local government.

We expected an early boost from the state of Pennsylvania to come our way through a $100,000 allocation from the capital budget. But release of that type of appropriation happens at the timing and discretion of the governor, and in the end, Governor Tom Ridge was appointed Director of Homeland Security, and the new governor decided not to release the funds. Our Congressman, John Peterson, did deliver on his promise to bring in a $100,000 grant through the Health Resources and Services Administration.

We created special giving opportunities that would enable people to feel connected with the new facilities and vision. These included benches, bricks, and a Wall of Fame, where local heroes could be honored for $10,000. The Wall of Fame was very successful, generating $210,000 for the campaign.

In the end, there were 904 community gifts overall. Fifty-three gifts of $5,000 or more from individual organizations and businesses totaled $1,153,435, and the rest—over 850 gifts total—were from small, local donations. We encouraged collaborations of all sorts and donations of all sizes. The largest individual donation was $189,000, and the smallest donation was $7. It was really a massive community effort of a type we had not pulled off in the town in some time, reminding me of the launch of the Arts Festival, which had drawn similarly on the university, local business people, and a team of intrepid volunteers.

People frequently said I was "tenacious" about this project. It's true that I became obsessed with the importance of LifeLink to the health and vitality of the whole community, and I would not rest until we surpassed our goal. But the real credit in any project of this scale goes to the volunteer committee who provided the horsepower and the board that provided oversight and direction every step of the way.

The ground-breaking was held in April 2003 in the pouring rain, and the new headquarters opened in December 2004. When we started the campaign, Alpha Ambulance had four ambulances and an exhausted team of twenty-five, still mostly volunteers. As of this writing, the Centre LifeLink EMS includes fifty paid employees along with fifty volunteers and operates a fleet of seven ambulances and four emergency vans.

CHAPTER 37
LEARN FROM OTHER WOMEN: *LUNCH WITH MIMI LIVE*

In 2004, when Kish Bank, based in Juniata and Mifflin Counties, decided to enter the Centre County market, president Bill Hayes made a cold call to my office to introduce himself. Bill is big and avuncular, the kind of guy who gets his way with humor, kindness, and persistence. I liked him right away.

"Everyone I talk to," he began, with a huge smile on his face, "everyone says be sure to call on Mimi." He invited me to serve on their local advisory board.

He was definitely not the first banker to pop that question, and I always refused. Long ago, when I was offered Sy's place on the Farmers National Bank board, I had decided never ever to serve on an auxiliary board. In my mind, it was only worth my time if I was really a director, not an advisor.

So, it should come as no surprise that I turned down the Kish Bank advisory board as well. We talked about a variety of other topics and left the door open to explore how I might help Kish Bank launch successfully in the Centre Region. At a lunch together a few weeks later, Bill asked if I'd consider being a spokesperson in the bank's advertising. Many banks were customers in other parts of the business: in our magazines, on our billboards, and with our promotional products and agency divisions. And I had learned long ago not to bite the hands that feed you.

Again, I said, "No. there is no way I could be interested."

Bill said the bank's goal was to connect with women seriously as community leaders and as potential customers. That idea intrigued me, so I promised Bill I would keep thinking about something we could do together that would benefit both of us and the community.

As you've figured out by now, I love challenges, especially

challenges where the payoff is helping other women. Jill Shockey, *Town & Gown* editor at that time, brought me an idea that seemed a great fit. She suggested we create a live version of my monthly interview feature in *Town & Gown*. She suggested we call it *Lunch with Mimi Live* and hold it in a public venue where tickets could be sold, and money could be raised for charities that supported women in the community.

I scheduled another lunch with Bill Hayes, and in early 2005, we entered into a simple agreement to work out the details of *Lunch with Mimi Live*. Our goal was to host two or three live programs a year with a focus on issues of interest to women.

At our kickoff event at the Nittany Lion Inn in June 2005, Bill and I sat on stage. He interviewed me about "Women Who Work" and introduced the bank's intention to bring together panels of local women, hosted by me, to discuss issues of interest to women and the community. For the first event, the bank charged $30 for the lunch program and gave a gift of $1,000 to Centre Volunteers in Medicine. The formula seemed to work, and we were on our way.

Over time, the audience grew from thirty-eight women at the first event to seventy-five to one hundred each time. The live format always brings out my best. And with the focus on complicated, sometimes thorny issues faced by real women, several times *Lunch with Mimi Live* created life-changing moments for participants, audience members, and me.

One particularly moving panel was about "Mothers and Daughters" with participants Linda Gall, State College volunteer extraordinaire; Sue Werner, president of the State College Board of Education; and c a local estate attorney. I shared my concern that I hadn't spent enough time with my daughters when they were young and that it prevented me from having the relationships I wanted to have with them now that they were adults.

"You can have everything you want in life," I quoted something I heard younger women say often. "You just shouldn't try to make yourself have it all at once."

Lesson #42: It is vitally important to put first the things that are most important to you; no one knows what that is except you.

During the discussion, Ashley had an "a-ha" moment. She welled up a bit talking about wanting to spend more time with her twin daughters before they were in high school. Not long after, Ashley's husband Charles, in a casual moment, thanked me. Ashley realized from our public discussion that she needed to resign her grueling position at law firm McQuaide Blasko to spend more time with her teenage daughters. After our conversation, she set up her own solo law practice, focusing on estate planning and working from a home office when necessary so she could better balance her roles as a mother and wife.

"That panel gave me the idea that I could step out of full-time work, and go back in later," Ashley explained. "Working from home helped my daughters see how and why my work was important to me. And it also gave me time with them as individuals when it was so important to their overall growth as young women."

Ashley recently called to thank me once again and to seek my advice on her next career move. She wanted to work in development at Penn State where she could take the experience she gained from work in estate planning and use that expertise to connect more donors with the university. I helped her find the right people to talk to at the university, and she has recently started a new job as Director of Major Gifts at the College of Earth and Mineral Science.

Over its eleven-year run, *Lunch with Mimi Live* contributed $14,400 to local nonprofits. I continue to be asked by regular attendees, "Hey, what happened to *Lunch with Mimi Live*? I miss it!"

The magic of *Lunch With Mimi Live*—should you want to imitate it—was creating a public forum for discussions that enabled individual women to see themselves, their work, and their families in new ways. This is so important as we continue to push, at every level, for better and more balanced lives with equal opportunity and equal pay for our work.

CHAPTER 38
FACING A PAINFUL REALITY: MY JOURNEY THROUGH DIVORCE

There was one time I almost died on my way to Rye Brook. I was on Interstate 80 East, just past the Delaware Water Gap into New Jersey, when my car, a red Oldsmobile convertible, hit a big rock which knocked out the chassis, the whole bottom of the car. I lost my brakes, lost my steering, and the car started spinning out of control. I felt the car spinning, and horns blew in every direction. I just let it go. I was sure I was going to die. And then the car gently hit the guardrail and stopped. And, as my life so often goes, one of my neighbors had seen it all happen and pulled over to help me.

***

The weekend of September 8, 2007, Sam's son and daughter-in-law, Neil and Michelle Fredman, visited us for the first time at our new home on Honors Lane in the Village at Penn State. We were looking forward to enjoying the Notre Dame football game with them from the President's box.

I remember I was walking with Michelle early Saturday morning when she asked, "What is it with Sam and Carolyn?" After a dramatic pause, she continued, "Now he has me doing free legal work for her on her purchase of a new apartment."

When I pressed her, Michelle explained that Carolyn's new apartment was just around the corner from our new apartment in White Plains. An alarm went off. Michelle's questions provided a wake-up call to a story that was about to unfold and would have a horrible, ugly ending.

I couldn't give Michelle a substantive answer, but like Sherlock

Holmes, I began to notice little things that cumulatively spelled trouble: cigarette ashes in the unflushed toilet in my bathroom, a lipstick that was not mine in the medicine cabinet, Prada bedroom slippers in the back of my closet, and a device used to relieve back pain in our freezer. Over a period of several weeks, I noticed that Carolyn's mail would appear from time to time on our kitchen island.

I confronted Sam, who insisted, "Mimi, I promise, it's all nothing."

I wanted to believe him, but each time I drove from State College to White Plains, the trip seemed to get longer. I lacked the spirit that made the trip worth it.

In my mind, things were spinning out of control; the story I told myself about the marriage switched from "love is grand" to "total disaster." Once I lost trust in Sam in the present, the past became clouded with suspicions, and I sank deeper and deeper into doubt.

***

I first met Carolyn, Sam's "other woman," a few months after I started dating Sam, at a pre-election rally in the fall of 1989. The Palmers had flown me to Westchester in their plane, and we landed in the midst of a storm that rocked the plane every which way.

Carolyn had been Sam's secretary at his law firm and before that a woman he'd helped through a sticky divorce. Carolyn reappeared many times, in many settings, over the years, from Passover seders to family BBQs, always on the list of people Sam bought presents for when we were on vacation. Whenever I asked, I was told I was crazy to even think that anything was wrong. This is a subtle form of gaslighting many men use to control and manipulate women. But I was also kidding myself: I had rushed into the marriage, and I rushed through life ignoring flaws in the relationship the whole time I was in it, until it all seemed to be a lie.

A time of reckoning appeared a month later when Sam was scheduled for cataract surgery. I had just had oral surgery myself and experienced complications in recovery. Sam suggested I stay home and take care of myself. Carolyn would pick him up and take him to surgery, he said, and his daughter-in-law Susan would pick him up and bring him home afterward. I would drive to New York later in the week, when we could recover together. It all sounded plausible and very generous.

Though I was a bit suspicious about everything related to Carolyn and sensed the bottom of the marriage falling out, I loved Sam and was worried about him. I called home a few hours after the surgery, and there was no answer. So, I called Susan to see how things had gone. She knew nothing about her assignment to pick him up after the surgery. In that moment, I knew.

I slammed down the phone, paused, and decided to call my children. First, I called Nan because I had already shared with her my suspicions about things going south with Sam.

"Mom," she blurted out, "if it were me, I'd pack a bag, get in my car, and head for White Plains as quickly as I could." I was still very tired from my oral surgery and unfit to travel so late in the day, but I shifted into high gear to depart after my morning meeting the next day.

When I told Sam my plans, he begged and pleaded with me to stay in State College.

"Mimi, I'm fine. Really. Let me rest up for a couple days, and I'll come to State College Sunday or Monday."

I called my driver, David Brown, and arranged to have him pick me up at the office at 11 a.m. the next day.

There I was, alone in our new retirement home in State College: devastated, defeated, and enraged. I was embarrassed, too. I had frequently, quietly suspected something was not right. It seemed odd how often Carolyn showed up at family occasions. It seemed particularly strange when she showed up, unannounced, to show off her grandchild or to report to Sam on domestic errands she had completed for him.

She phoned often to check in at our home in Rye Brook. Once, when I questioned her motive under my breath before I had completely hung up the phone, she immediately called back asking, "What did you mean by those comments?"

"Just what I said," I replied and hung up.

The next morning, as I was preparing to leave, I got a call from Sam, again insisting that I recover at home and he'd come to State College by Monday. But I stuck to my guns.

"I'm leaving for White Plains at 11 a.m.," I said.

Suddenly, from the background I heard, "Why don't you tell her we have other plans?"

I wanted to go berserk but kept my cool.

"I'll see you mid-afternoon," I told him.

He called again when I was in the car. There was more pleading: "Please Mimi, your health comes first! I can explain everything to you. I'll be there Sunday or Monday."

In between the hideous calls back and forth with Sam while we were driving, Dave confessed that he had warned Sam, more than a few times, that he was "playing with fire" each time he delivered Sam to Carolyn's apartment complex when driving him back from State College.

"Thanks, Dave, for telling me now!"

I was sinking, drip by drip, into a dark world I had never encountered before. I felt trapped, deeply hurt, hopeless, helpless, and harassed--in very murky and frightening territory. Tick tock, tick tock, my spirit clock was losing time, maybe even running out. Despite my best efforts, I felt myself slipping, slowly into a mad woman's rage. Nothing could stop me from my mission to scream at him, at her, at myself for being so stupid and failing to see the writing on the wall for so many years.

On my way, I called my daughter Carol who urged me to take care of myself and remain calm.

"If you need me, I can be there in an hour. Just say so." Once we arrived, I asked Dave to wait in the lobby. At that point, I wasn't sure if I was staying or leaving.

I had an ultimatum to deliver: Sam must agree to a family meeting with all of our children that day or the next, or I would not stay. After considerable, ugly bickering, Sam finally agreed to talk to his children with me. Both of his sons and one of their wives came over that night to be informed about the situation and to discuss where we go from here.

We discussed immediate conditions and actions required. Sam agreed to go over to Carolyn's apartment, just a few blocks away, to retrieve his personal belongings and tell her that the relationship was over. By this point, my mind was foggy from depression, and though the evidence was everywhere, it took me a long time to connect the dots.

The next morning, Saturday, after a restless night, I woke up an out-of-control, defeated woman. I felt tingles under my skin, running up my arms, an unrelenting anger and sadness, a darker cloud over me than I had ever experienced before. My rage was triggered again and again as I walked through the apartment seeing what I'd missed before: Carolyn's traces were everywhere, including her silk negligee at the bottom of my underwear drawer.

Sam called his son, Andy, who came right over to help. I called Carol and Nan and alerted both of them on my state of mind. Carol and her husband, Jed, came to help us immediately with the next steps. Jed, who is a doctor, called New York Hospital, Westchester County, and arranged an emergency psychiatric consult for me.

The psychiatrist, a sweet man appropriately named Angel, said it was safe for me to go home, so long as someone stayed with me. After that evaluation, we decided to hold a joint family meeting the next day at Neil and Michelle's home. Michelle talked more than either of the boys at that meeting. It felt to me like she was trying to sympathize with Sam's side and even justify his infidelity.

I reluctantly agreed to have Sam return with me to State College, and we briefly tried to reconcile. But by then, I couldn't stand his presence.

He woke up Monday morning, after my dark and sleepless night, and announced, "You treat me like shit."

"And, how do you treat me?" I asked. "You can't be trusted. The sooner you leave, the better. It's over!" I had not spoken with an attorney; I just knew in my heart I could not make it work any longer.

***

On the day before Valentine's Day, 2008, Sam received notice of my intention to file for divorce from a county delivery boy. He left the next day and readied himself for battle. My husband, an experienced matrimonial lawyer, knew all the tricks. He had written our prenup. He had paid for all the furnishings in our new house. In many other subtle ways, he had set himself up to triumph in this exact situation. I was a novice dealing with a situation that overwhelmed me and pushed me to the edge of despair.

Again and again, Sam's lawyer did all he could to destroy my will and reduce me to tears, but my experience overcoming bigger adversity than this carried me through the horrible, demeaning ordeal.

When I learned how much I'd have to pay Sam for the divorce settlement, I imagined it would be fun to deliver it in pennies. When I called my friends at Kish Bank to learn how much that would weigh—over two and a half tons—I shared my scandalous idea with my financial advisor, and she offered to come with me in the truck to deliver it, dumping it in the front yard at the hotel where he maintained his residence in Harrison, New York.

My attorney almost passed out when I told him.

"Mimi, it's over!" he said. "You really did better than we all expected."

Make no mistake: divorce brings out the worst in all parties. The details are ugly and not worth repeating. In the end, the six-figure check I was ordered to pay my ex was the best one I ever signed. On the memo line I wrote: "Reward for infidelity." November 27, 2010 became a symbol of a new, even more stimulating time in my life as I tiptoed into retirement, free to be me and live life as I pleased.

***

Though infidelity was the death knell, our marriage was doomed to failure because we both needed to be in charge. We had no way to negotiate the many little challenges that are a natural part of any relationship, and when we met we were both in agonizing pain from previous losses.

And because of our age difference—I was fifty-seven, and he was sixty-seven—I was still at the height of my energy and health, and he was visibly declining. On a typical Sunday, he would read the paper and watch sports on TV. I preferred to visit one of the kids or go to a museum or concert. I felt I was still striving, while he was resting on his laurels.

It was a sign of my overall lack of trust in Sam that we had never established a joint checking account. I had always kept my funds separate from his. I started drinking a lot in those years, one of the ways I avoided dealing with how limited the relationship really was. Almost as soon as our lightning courtship and magical wedding were over, we began growing apart. We loved one another and loved many of the same things, but our relationship was always rocky and contested. I was more subservient in that relationship than I'd ever been before. Sam really didn't like Carol—because she openly challenged him—and I let Sam's discomfort limit the amount of time I spent with Carol and her children, something I will always regret.

Even under the best of circumstances, a commuter relationship is very hard to sustain. It requires a kind of compromise, flexibility, and trust that had made my relationship with Lou stronger, but I could not generate those traits between me and Sam.

Lesson #43: Being alone allows vital time for introspection. One of the great gifts of aging is having that time and the ability to look at life from many different perspectives.

When you jump into things without thinking them through and then stick with them out of habit, you can land in big, complicated messes that may seem acceptable at the time, but that you come to regret later. The Towers. Marriage to Sam Fredman. Shutting Carol out of my life for nearly two decades because she frightened me. All of these things I had to confront and work through in the 2000s came from rash decisions I'd made right after Lou's death and clung to fiercely for the next decade.

Looking back, I could have prevented so much pain to myself and others, if I'd taken more time to slow down and think things through after Lou died. Sy helped me do that. Lou helped me do that. When the divorce finally happened, I was more than ready to slow down and reclaim ownership of my time and choices once again. But it took several rocky years to get there.

CHAPTER 39
ASKING FOR A DIFFERENT KIND OF HELP: MY DEPRESSION DIAGNOSIS AND RECOVERY

For diabetes, I take a couple pills daily, watch my diet, and exercise daily for effective results. For declining eyesight, I take eye vitamins twice a day, use a magnifying glass to read the smaller type, and get regular checkups for early macular degeneration in one of my eyes. And for my bit of hearing loss, I amplify sound with my hearing aids.

I'm a woman of action, and almost nothing stands in my way when I'm intent to conquer something, even in myself. But for the first seventy-plus years of my life, I vigorously avoided talking to anyone—even my closest friends—about my recurring symptoms of depression. It was not until my third marriage fell apart that I finally took my moods and emotions seriously and began seeking treatment for the sometimes-debilitating anxiety and despair I had come to take for granted as part of my everyday life.

As I began to claw my way out of the pit of depression that plagued me after I discovered Sam's infidelity, Carol and Nan became a real source of support for me. Carol showed me some very simple yoga poses to get me through my most challenging moments. And one pivotal night, after I'd spent several weeks isolated and alone, she helped me get dressed, so I could go to the opening of the new State Theater.

Here's what my depression looked like: I would wake up at 3 a.m. Unable to sleep, I'd drive downtown to my office. I'd stare at my desk, but I couldn't work. I'd come back to the house, sit at the kitchen table, and try to work there. Unable to start anything, I'd go back to bed. But I couldn't sleep. I was crippled emotionally. I had this strange feeling under the skin of my hands and arms that wouldn't go away. It didn't hurt; it tingled. Now, whenever that feeling returns, I stop in my tracks and try to figure out what is bothering me—literally under my skin. I calm myself down by working or walking or just sitting quietly and appreciating all that life has given me.

But in the fall of 2007, none of that was working. As my third marriage fell apart, I was heading toward a crash landing. My recovery from oral surgery was not progressing properly. I was building up quiet anxiety about my decision to sell my business, and my relationships between and among Carol and Nan showed increasing signs of conflict and dysfunction. Absolutely nothing in my life felt like it was going right.

One Sunday morning, I awakened with a feeling of impending doom. I could find no comfortable place or position to sit or to lay down. I walked around my home in circles, surrounded by a cloud of despair. I knew I needed help. But I feared the consequences of calling either Carol or Nan. They each lived more than three hours away, and I didn't want to disrupt their lives. If I told one of them, I had to tell both of them, and then I'd be exposed to their bitter fighting. My best friend Barb was on an extended trip to Morocco with other friends.

I knew my family doctor from Hershey was at a swimming meet at the University of Pennsylvania where his older son was competing. I tiptoed quietly to my medicine cabinet and considered an overdose of aspirin, the way my older sister Sylvia had ended her own life at age fifty-three. The weight of life felt too much to carry. I had no place to turn. Tears begin to drip down my cheeks. As I opened the medicine cabinet, I looked at myself in the mirror and slammed the door shut.

"Oh crap, what am I doing?" I said out loud. "Stop! Get help! Don't be stupid, Mimi!"

I propped up my bed pillows and tried to shift into survival mode.

"You can do this Mimi. But you need *help*. Who can help you here and now?"

Only days before, I had attended an evening meeting at Dr. Jon Dranov's home. The hospital administrators and board members were recruiting leadership for a capital campaign for the hospital expansion. He was a casual acquaintance, and people said he was the best doctor in town. Sy had been part of the team that had recruited him to Centre County years ago. My mind was foggy and confused. My body was numb but tingling. All of this thinking took hours on the clock. By the time it was 11 a.m., I wondered if I could call him. Maybe he could help me get myself on track. Back and forth, back and forth, I talked to myself.

Finally, near noon, I gathered the courage to call and seek help from a doctor I had never seen as a patient—at his home on a Sunday, no less, definitely not my usual style. Luckily, his wife, Judy, answered.

I identified myself and confessed, "I'm sorry to call, but I'm in need of help. Is John available?"

"Yes, he's working in the garden. I'll go get him," she said.

"What can I do for you, Mimi?" he asked.

"I'm experiencing a terrible anxiety attack. I feel like I'm trapped. No place to go. Thinking of destroying myself. Enough is enough. Can you help me?"

"I'll try. Tell me a little more," he warmly requested. His voice was soothing, the pace tuned to my fragile state. Immediately, I opened up and trusted him.

"I can't stay still. There's no comfortable place to sit or lay down. I'm not sleepy or hungry. There's a terrible tingling under my skin and up my arms. I have no zest for life. The air is out of my balloon, and I feel ready to end it all. I can't accept it. It's just too much for me to handle. Sorry to dump this on you, but I need…help! I can't stand it."

"Before I can prescribe anything, you'll need some blood work," he replied. "Get yourself to the hospital emergency room. I'll call ahead and alert them and order the tests. After they phone the results to me, I'll be able to order a prescription that you can pick up later today. Who's your pharmacy? Call my office in the morning to schedule an appointment so that I can do a thorough checkup tomorrow," he instructed.

How I managed to get dressed and get myself to the hospital, I'm unable to tell you. I was so paralyzed from head to toe. I was whisked into the lab upon arrival and received a phone call from Dranov thirty-five minutes after I arrived back home. I was spread out on my unmade king-sized bed. He instructed me to pick up my prescription at Wegmans.

"Don't hesitate to call me if you need me before I see you tomorrow. Be good to yourself."

"Thank you," I said as I hung up, tears running down my cheeks.

"Sure, be good to myself. I have no energy for that either," I said out loud into my empty bedroom. Tomorrow seemed too far to reach.

In the past when I was in a "bad, bad mood," I'd just dig more deeply into my work. I called it "my therapy," and often when I was most glum, I'd jump into action and produce my best, most creative work. But this time, I could neither work nor sit still. I was seventy-four, utterly alone, and falling apart.

My appointment with Dranov early the next afternoon became the beginning of the rest of my life. He helped me get my physical health back on track, and he convinced me that I needed to see a psychiatrist to help my recovery. He prescribed pills to help me beat down the anxiety, but he insisted that by themselves, the pills wouldn't work.

The doctor he recommended, Timothy Derstine ('97), had a long waiting list. He said I might have to wait a few weeks to see him, but he believed he was the most competent psychiatrist in the area, so he assured me the delay would be worth it.

For someone who grew up with the idea that only "crazy" people needed psychiatric help, this was a major jump for me. But jump I did. I told myself that I wasn't crazy, but I knew I had a lot of baggage to unpack and unload in order to get back to a life worth living.

But, oh, I was so nervous before that first therapy session in January 2008. Sam and I had made one last attempt at seeing whether we were capable of having a good time together. We flew with the Penn State alumni trip to the Alamo Bowl as part of the official party. To put it bluntly, it was pure hell for me. I was actually embarrassed to be with him. I saw only his flaws: obesity, incessant talking, excessive eating, drunkenness, his self-centered nature and the way he always stretched the truth. That trip confirmed my need to end the marriage, but I needed all sorts of help to get me through that ugly process.

My very first appointment with Derstine, he had already done some homework, which really impressed me. He informed me that his preference was to work as a team with a social worker, Mary Sroka, who was, coincidentally, a native of Johnstown, where I spent my life as the commuter-wife of Senator W. Louis Coppersmith. If I had any privacy objections, he could try to find someone else, but he preferred to collaborate with her. The decision was mine to make. I hadn't met her, but I knew her parents, Marion and John, and had no objection whatsoever.

At first, I was very tentative about the whole therapy experience. Would I have the capacity to let it all hang out? How could I avoid holding back? Did I have the strength to open up and allow my "ghosts" out of captivity?

Derstine was tall but soft-spoken and understated. His office had a desk—behind which he sat, a couch and two chairs on the other side of the desk. I sat in one of the chairs across from him. I had no idea what to expect, but his questions were clear, concise, and rational, which calmed my insecurity.

I started at the beginning and shared my early years as a bed-wetter through all the little things along the way that I felt had contributed to my complex, crowded, and confusing lifestyle, including the many losses that were each singular moments that shaped my life overall, as well as my emotional limitations.

Therapy has been, for me, a life-enhancing journey and an opportunity for real self-improvement. I still go at least once a month, I like to say, "Just to get the air in my tires checked."

Derstine asks simple-yet-direct questions that lead to at least partial solutions to complex relationships. The biggest most challenging issues, over this decade of therapy, have been the relationships of my daughters with one another and with me.

I feel that I have learned to more clearly define and express my needs in a non-threatening style. My life's circumstances provided great opportunity for me to excel in business and public service and to keep things together for many people. Therapy helped me identify the risks I'd created in delegating the care of my children to others during their most formative years and challenging events. I gave them material comfort but did not know how to make them feel emotionally safe. If I had to do it over again, I believe I would reorder those priorities.

Lesson #44: In life, you don't get do-overs, and so it is essential that you also learn to forgive yourself for all the things you did not know how to do or give.

I have gained deep respect for the tangible value and practical help of psychiatry and psychotherapy. It has enhanced the quality of my own life as well as that of my friends and family. It was, perhaps, the hardest type of help I ever had to ask for, but also the one that has helped me the most.

CHAPTER 40
SELLING MY BUSINESS: A NEW BEGINNING

Back in the late 1970s, when I attended a Beta Sigma Rho homecoming event, alumnus Arnold Hoffman ('59), an investment banker with Lehman Brothers, asked me, "You own a billboard company, don't you?"

"Yes, I do," I answered.

"Well, if you're ever thinking of selling it, give me a call. I've worked with several companies in the industry. Here's my card."

"I may need you someday," I said at the time, tucking his card in my wallet. Over the years, I'd noticed the card from time to time when I cleaned out my wallet.

I pulled it out in November, 2007, shortly after my final ugly commute to White Plains, as I thought through my options. I had to face the realities: I was almost seventy-five years old. I had no viable succession plan in my family or among my employees, and at the time, I was sunk in a deep depression with little interest in the future.

Though I had no idea what the future would bring, on any front, I knew in my heart it was time for me to get on with the rest of my life. Once I made the decision, I reached out to Arnold Hoffman to set the sale of my business—Morgan Signs, Inc. doing business as The Barash Group—in motion. I had started the sale of the business before the divorce, so technically the sale of the business counted as marital assets. Though this would be a costly decision, because of my depression and overall exhaustion, I felt I needed to push forward, at once, with both the divorce and the sale of the business.

Arnold and I had our first meeting at the Nittany Lion Inn, and I left with a punch list of directions and a target date for each key item on the list. I apprised our General Manager, Dick Hall, so he could help me prepare all the materials for a follow-up meeting at the Bob

Evans Restaurant, just off the Pennsylvania Turnpike, in Swatara Township near Harrisburg.

At that meeting, we talked about the major prospects for purchase and Arnold suggested that we give the best prospect—Lamar Advertising, our chief competitor—an opportunity for a preemptive bid, which challenges the prospect to give their best bid within thirty days in exchange for our giving them exclusive first rights to bid. We would offer the company to no other prospects unless we turned down their bid.

To my complete amazement and joy, Lamar's preemptive bid was fifty percent greater than my highest imagined price. When Arnold called me that evening in late November, I was asleep, though it was still early. I was still having trouble sleeping from the depression and the likely prospect of divorce. The news of a reliable New York Stock Exchange traded company offering me top dollar for a company I'd started with my first husband in the basement of our first home filled me with hope. News of the imminent sale buoyed me through the next few months and helped give me the courage to divorce Sam. We scheduled the closing for January 31, 2008, the forty-ninth anniversary of the day Sy and I started the business.

I experienced how really big deals work. First, Lamar had a month to do due diligence: tons of paperwork, follow-up details, high-powered—and high priced—legal and accounting work to achieve the close. I worked hard to help key employees transition to the new owners and to assist others in finding new jobs. We helped all the employees with the transfer of their benefits, including 401(k) and profit sharing accounts we had helped them fund over the years.

After we sold Morgan Signs to Lamar, we still owned the publications and agency divisions. These were smaller and potentially more complicated transactions that required me in the trenches for another six months. In the case of the agency, I decided to give those client relationships to our two top artists, Skip Webster and Chip Mock. They opted to set up separate businesses and divided the clients between them, giving each client the choice to stay with Skip or Chip. Both of them are still in business, as of this writing, going strong almost a decade later.

The last asset to go was Barash Media and its anchor product, *Town & Gown*, which we sold to The Gazette Printers, from Indiana, Pennsylvania, which owns several other local publications and introduced the *Centre County Gazette*, a weekly paper to the region. For ten years, I have stayed on as a consultant to *Town & Gown*. I'm so proud of the way *Town & Gown* has stood the test of truly competitive times for print publications without me running the day-to- day business.

And I am delighted that another first-generation Penn State alumna, Vilma Shu Danz, has taken over as the head of Barash Media. With this shift, I know that *Town & Gown* is in great hands for the future. I see *Town & Gown* as my legacy, something I've nourished for over fifty years against stiff competition and years of barely breaking even. As I reflect on my total work effort, I must confess that the lowest profit-makers often provided my greatest joy and satisfaction. *Town & Gown* made me rich in a way that may be remembered and built upon when I am gone.

CHAPTER 41
THE BUSINESS OF A CURE: THINK PINK EN ROUTE TO PINK ZONE

The Pink Zone is my payback for the privilege of surviving breast cancer. I'm driven to make it successful because of my passion to be sure that women from all backgrounds have access to breast cancer survival.

In 2006, when Greg Myford ('86), Penn State Associate Director of Intercollegiate Athletics, asked me to sponsor the first "Think Pink" Lady Lion Basketball game, I was an eighteen-year-survivor of breast cancer. And I'd been a passionate supporter of Lady Lion Basketball since Rene Portland assumed the reins as head coach in 1980. So for me, it was a no-brainer; I contributed $3,500. The NCAA provided a one-time grant of $5,000 to encourage special events for breast cancer research and to help build the fanbase for women's intercollegiate basketball.

Rene came up with the idea to use the NCAA gift to stage a "Think Pink" game to raise money for cancer research and to honor breast cancer survivors in Central Pennsylvania. The Lady Lions were the first to wear pink uniforms and originated the idea of honoring survivors, as part of the overall effort to raise awareness about cancer. For that first game, $20,000 was raised, as fans poured into the Bryce Jordan Center, and thirty survivors from the community were honored at half-time.

The next year, I increased my support to $5,000 and joined some of the meetings with the volunteers who had become more involved. After I sold my business in 2008, and around the time the NCAA changed the name nationally to Pink Zone, this became one of my key philanthropic efforts. We registered as "Pennsylvania Pink Zone" because I believed a twelve-month, statewide effort was most likely to succeed. I felt I had the capacity to bring in larger donations, increase visibility locally and nationally, and raise overall awareness about scientific research.

In the early years, most of the money went out of town to the Susan G. Komen Cancer Fund and the Pennsylvania Breast Cancer Coalition. Working to expand our volunteer base beyond the university and to engage local survivors and activists, it became clear to me that we would get further in our fund-raising if there was a local hook.

Lesson #45: Knowing your audience and speaking directly to them gains more powerful results.

Joel Diamond ('76), a former Lewistown business owner and the ticket manager for Penn State Athletics, proposed that we engage area hospitals both for help with fundraising and also as beneficiaries of our efforts. This idea clicked, and we were off and running to rapid growth.

At this point, in addition to the overall leadership committee, we set up a separate fundraising committee to build sponsorships, to solicit more individuals for personal gifts at all levels, and to develop other fundraising opportunities. A student committee, chaired by Eric Bodner, sprung into action as well. Central to student efforts was a fundraising letter to parents and the sale of t-shirts and other wearables promoting the Pink-Zone. The sale of official pink t-shirts converted the area to a sea of pink, like the famous Penn State football "white out."

For the first couple years, we ran the Pink Zone entirely on volunteer energy, hiring our first executive director, Miriam Powell, in 2010. She later became an employee of Lady Lion Basketball in 2016. Miriam's steadfast, groundbreaking leadership accelerated our capacity to grow in hefty incremental stages. With revenue from t-shirts sales, special events, ticket sales, parking, and both live and silent online auctions, we grew to a high of $300,000 in 2016, distributed to five different agencies, including Mount Nittany Health, where we were able to add more mammogram machines, open a lounge for family members to gain more information, and hire a breast cancer patient navigator, the role that had been so important to me in overcoming the huge challenge of breast cancer twenty years before.

When I discovered a lump in my breast in 1989, I was lucky in every possible way: I found the lump early; through my role as a Penn State trustee, I had access to the best cancer treatment available; and I had Nancy Toth to talk me through my options and help me figure out what was right for me. The thread that runs through everything that make me truly happy is making it possible for other people to be as lucky: to receive a great education, to access world-class health care, and to live in a community where you are valued and able to thrive as who you are.

It all started on July 25, 1945, when we received the telegram that my brother had died. I read the telegram with my own eyes, I took it in, and out of the chaos and pain, I chose to help others. I have been re-reading and responding to that telegram my entire life.

Lesson #46: Whether your drive comes from faith or family, work or volunteer initiatives, there are opportunities every day to make a real, measurable difference.

CHAPTER 42
THE POWER OF FRIENDSHIP: LIVING AND LEARNING WITH BARB PALMER

When Sy and I moved to 325 Homan Avenue in 1956, Jim and Barb Palmer had already been living on the street for three years. At that time, there were no sidewalks, no sewers, and the street was not yet paved up to our block. Jim had an architect design the house and then built it himself with subcontractors. The kitchen was at the front of the house. The prep sink faced the street, and Barb looked up and waved when we drove by.

Jim had been a young engineer, working with Penn State professors to build rooftop amplifiers for cable television. At that time, there was only one TV station received in State College, so they were solving a real, local problem.

Barb and Jim's daughter, Jan, roamed across the street one afternoon, and we got to know her first. In 1959, when Sy bought out the advertising and billboard business from Sid Friedman and we moved our business to the basement of that house, the back door was never locked. It was the entrance to both the kitchen and the downstairs office. Jan walked in the side door and down the back stairs to the office. I was at the layout table doing ads. She wanted to know what I was doing so I explained.

Then I asked her, "What does your father do?" I knew, but she told me, in great detail, about Centre Video. I said, "Let's play a little and do some ads for your dad's company."

The next night, I arrived home from a meeting of my sorority, where I was the advisor. Jim and Sy were sitting on the floor of our unfurnished living room talking about the ads Jan and I made together. That was the beginning of a long and sometimes rocky business relationship, in which I learned a lot not just about advertising and marketing, but about cable television. Working for Jim, we had the wonderful experience of seeing cable television grow from the ground up. We met forward-looking scientists and engineers in the Palmers' circle, and though on the surface we seemed very different from one another, Barb and I became close friends, through thick and thin, pushing one another in important new directions.

Jim had learned to fly, so he could get in and out of small towns in Pennsylvania more quickly than was possible by car. Barb took flying lessons and became a pilot as well. She was quite involved in the local community, and she ran the local Girl Scout troupe when Jan was a member. Barb and Jim were leaders of a group that formed a second, smaller offshoot of the Presbyterian Church downtown, called Diakonia.

One of the toughest and most creative people I ever met, Jim was hard on Barb and his children, pushing them all to excel. Somehow Barb took it all in; she was a rock for him and the children. She cooked lavish meals, trying new things all the time. When Sy's mother sent us a frozen Shabbat meal on a Friday night (she sent them Special Delivery through the U.S. Postal Service in the days before FedEx)—with a whole roasted chicken, soup and everything to go with it--we'd often take it over to the Palmers and share it with them. That was one of Barb's few reprieves from making a lavish dinner every night.

Barb and I shared a very strong sense of duty and community service, of doing the right thing even when it may not be the easy or popular thing. Once, in the 1970s, through the church, Barb took in a young woman from Baltimore who was pregnant until she had her child and returned back home. When Sy became ill, Barb and Jim stepped up in so many ways, large and small, to help us through. They flew us in their private plane to New York. When both Sy and I were in the hospital on Carol's sixteenth birthday, Barb served Carol and her friends a fondue dinner, sitting around the coffee table, on her living room floor. And when Sy fell down in the bedroom on the morning of February 8, 1975, Carol called Barb and Jim to come quickly across the street. When the EMTs arrived, Barb was giving Sy CPR.

But the real power of our friendship blossomed in the 2000s, after Jim died of kidney cancer and especially during and after my divorce. When I was struggling with depression, Barb insisted that I move closer to her. She would make sure I got moving in the morning; she'd take me out for walks in the afternoon; and she provided a much-needed judgement-free zone where I could talk about anything that was on my mind and know that it was safe with her.

After Sam and I separated, Barb and I began taking educational trips together, including extended visits to Chautauqua, New York, the Crystal Bridges Art Museum in Bentonville, Arkansas, and numerous cruises all around the world. Together, we sponsored a student in Musical Theater at Penn State, and we both buy two tickets to every concert, sporting event, and lecture. If one of us can't go, we take someone else, but we keep getting out, keep meeting new people, keep learning and growing from one another and the community.

Like me, Barb is a cancer survivor, and she has struggled valiantly to overcome the challenges of that illness and the normal effects of aging. As I finish this book, Barb is visibly declining. When Carol and I sat with her to read parts of the book to her and gather in her memories, what she could remember was limited. There are things each of us knows about the other that no one else knows, and there is a thread of making sure the other person is never alone, no matter what, that has kept us together through the most painful of personal times.

Barb was with me through every bit of the divorce drama.

She once said, "Keep me away from him. If I'm able, I'll kick him down the stairs for you."

Of course, she was exaggerating, but it was very important for me to hear that at the time and know that when I left the courtroom, I could be myself. I was not alone.

When Sy was dying, I was so busy taking care of the business that I missed his last days and weeks, something I've struggled to make up for as I get older and my friends get sick and die. It has been painful watching Barb's decline, sitting with her as she struggles to finish the most basic tasks and wondering if she has the stamina to go on. Barring some catastrophe, I will likely outlive her, and I am ready for that—as ready as anyone can be to lose someone who has been a friend through sixty years of husbands and children; businesses started, grown, and sold; and the daily conversations that are the most important part of each person's life.

To watch someone you love and admire decline and suffer from the frustration of not always being able to get her brain to function creates indescribable pain and conflict for me. On the one hand, I want to push her and help her find the words that escape her. On the other hand, I don't want to add to her frustration. It's extremely challenging to find the correct path to follow, but I remain motivated, encouraging her to maintain a vision of today as worthwhile and meaningful despite the physical and emotional pain.

My favorite times with Barb have come through our shared public leadership. Recently, in the process of discussing the new Discovery Space Museum in State College, I suggested that it would be exciting to introduce children to art side-by-side activities designed to activate their love of STEM.

We talked about the idea over dinner and Barb said, "You know I could lend them one of our family's sculptures, one that the children could touch." Presto! The first thing children see and experience in the new museum is that sculpture.

Together we make things happen that neither of us would have thought of alone. In this sense, I'm reminded of the creative energy and friendship I shared with both Sy and Lou. With Barb, I also share our experience as daughters, wives, mothers, grandmothers, and widows. We came of age and we are aging in times of extraordinary change in the lives of women and girls. We love being the grandmothers of the community, as it were, setting new things in motion that will benefit future generations.

For as long as it lasts, I am content to take her out in her wheelchair, help her caregivers navigate the events she can go to, and help her work through the exhaustion the day after one of those outings. I will miss Barb dearly when she is gone. In the meantime, I pick up her prescriptions, bring her favorite foods for dinner, and learn to sit patiently as she struggles to sit up, to breathe, and to gather her stamina for yet one more day. I am grateful for each one, exactly as it comes.

CHAPTER 43
ANYTHING IS STILL POSSIBLE: THE BELLEFONTE MUSEUM

Over the course of my life, I've had the opportunity to know and work with dozens of women, some paid and many volunteers, who have left an extraordinary impact on this community. For many years, when my life was consumed with business, my most important daily relationships were with other business people—and in those days, they were often men.

One of the real joys of my later years has been the opportunity to spend more time with women whose friendships have helped me discover so many things about myself. I've had wonderful experiences with them—from dinners to movies to exploring nature and the arts. I feel that this is a new part of my role as a woman and a citizen, helping women of all ages follow their visions and connecting them with people who can help them do it.

I do not feel I am particularly talented at the nuts and bolts of relationships—that's something Barb excels at—but I do know when to call on people to go a bit outside their comfort zone to make something nearly impossible happen. And I still love the feeling when we have all gone, individually, in a bit of a new direction and together discovered some new realm where we can have an impact together.

In that sense I'm still a catalyst.

Lesson #47: The most surprising things can happen under the right, friendly environment.

One great example is the Bellefonte Art Museum of Centre County. When Patricia House, an experienced curator and museum director from California, decided to relocate back east, near her son and daughter-in-law and their children in 2007, she chose Bellefonte, the county seat as her home.

She admired the beauty and history of the nineteenth-century downtown, which had been added to the National Registry of Historic Places in the 1970s, along with a number of other places throughout Bellefonte: the Bellefonte Armory, Brockerhoff Hotel, the County Court House, Gamble Mill, the Pennsylvania Match Factory, and many of the original Victorian mansions now turned into bed-and-breakfasts.

Against that backdrop, House began to talk about her idea of creating a county Art Museum in downtown Bellefonte to nurture local artists and local history and to help promote Bellefonte as a tourist destination. She discovered and became particularly interested in the architecture of Anna Wagner Keichline (1881-1943), a native of Bellefonte who attended Penn State, graduated from Cornell, and was the first female architect certified in Pennsylvania. She is known primarily for innovations in kitchen design that would save women time and labor—including the first combination sink and wash tub—and for inventing K-brick, a lighter and stronger material for building foundations. She also led a suffragette march in Bellefonte in 1913 and served as a special agent and spy in World War I.

A history of Keichline's work was one of the opening exhibits at the Bellefonte Art Museum when it opened in 2007. Most of the Museum's exhibits change monthly, offering over 150 local artists opportunities to display their work and meet one another. When the museum was just getting off the ground, Judy Sieg, wife of local real estate entrepreneur Phil Sieg, who gave me sage business advice after Lou's death, became the lead investor and catalyst for the museum's growth. Judy invited me and Barb to lunch at her house and asked us to become early supporters of the museum.

Those early gifts allowed House to restore and remodel the John Blair Linn House as the Museum's home. In the process of renovating the Linn House, she discovered a secret room that reinforced local rumors about the house as a station on the Underground Railroad. The Linn House was, in fact, a very early site for the Underground Railroad, operating as early as the 1830s. There was, at that time, a vibrant free black community in Bellefonte, along with many Quaker abolitionists, who had moved to the area as farmers in the 1790s. The Museum houses a permanent exhibition about key role of the house, and several other homes and churches in and around Bellefonte, in the abolition movement.

In addition to local history and local artists' exhibits that change monthly, the museum offers adult and children's art classes, summer art camps, storytelling, poetry, music, and a wide range of educational events meant to enrich the lives of locals as well as visitors. The Museum boasts more than five hundred members—a huge number in Central Pennsylvania—as well as eighty-six volunteers and over seven thousand visitors annually. All of this from the vision of one woman to bring more art and history to downtown Bellefonte: a remarkable example of how women and communities can work together for the greater good.

AFTERWORD
THE POSSIBILITY OF MIRACLES

Last Thanksgiving, November 2016, Carol and I were having breakfast at her kitchen table. I had just taken my bone density pill and was waiting twenty minutes to have breakfast before heading home.

She asked, "Mom, what are your big plans for 2017?"

I swallowed the last of my water and said, "I'd really like to finish my book."

"You know," she smiled, "that's what I do. I've helped other women CEOs write and publish their stories. I could help you... I'd love to help you..." The end of her sentence trailed off as we both remembered so many years of struggle between us. But, miraculously, at that moment, we were both ready. We had both been working for more than a decade with our separate therapists and in our time together to create something meaningful and real in the present.

By the end of that conversation, we agreed to meet at least once a month throughout 2017, and Carol promised to do "whatever it takes" to help me finish the book I'd started in 1989, after Lou died, and had never finished, though I'd tried three times with three different editors over the past twenty-five years.

Carol sent me home with her 10 x 10 exercise, to explore the moments that had defined my life, decade by decade. By the time she arrived in State College in January for our first weekend together, I had one legal pad for each decade, plus files and notes sprawled all over my study.

At first, I was finishing a book I called *Lunch with Mimi*, which brought together the best interviews I'd conducted for *Town & Gown* over the years, plus forty-eight new ones I conducted for the book. For each decade, I had also started to write "anecdotes," big a-ha moments in my personal and professional growth. But when we started I was still thinking of myself primarily as the editor of other people's stories.

When Carol asked me for details of my own life, again and again I told her, "I really don't think that other people will be interested in my story."

"I'm interested, Mom," she said. "Let's get it out on paper. You can decide what you want to do with it later."

Carol and I went back into those anecdotes—many of which were set pieces I told frequently in speeches and everyday conversation—and she helped me bring them to life. She would ask me probing questions and type quickly while I answered, capturing my exact words. In that process the stories went from my formal written voice to the more playful tone of everyday conversation, which is where I have always felt most comfortable myself. Carol asked me about my personal history, starting with my early years as a student, as a wife, and as a mother. We worked through decade by decade. And what we produced really felt and sounded like me.

A couple months into our project, Carol let me in on a secret: "You know, I was really afraid I wouldn't be able to do this. But then I thought to myself, 'If I ran into this woman at a party, I'd be really interested and want to spend time with her.' So at first, I pretended you weren't my mother. You were just an interesting woman I'd met at a party, and I was getting to know you all over again."

We laughed; we cried; and then we went out to eat... over and over, at my home in State College and at Carol's home in South Orange, New Jersey, across many months. We created an imaginary reader—a young woman in her thirties or forties looking for inspiration to get through a big challenge—and Carol asked me the questions she thought that reader would want to know about me. It was all very easy and natural. Years of bickering and self-doubt faded to the background, and I came to really long for the time I spent with Carol, learning about her and learning about myself.

I started to share our work with my closest friends, and what they were most interested in was not the interviews of other people, but my own stories. I had a particularly moving conversation with Anne Palmer, who helped me see that I had two books fighting with one another. She also encouraged me to keep going with the personal anecdotes.

"I find you really inspiring, Mimi," she said. "If you can bottle that, you will help a lot of young women get through the things that you had to get through."

That idea kept me going, and eventually, I let the interviews fade into the background. I changed the title to *Eat First, Cry Later*, to reflect my mother's no-nonsense approach to life and my deeply rooted Jewish background.

The process was not without challenges. When Carol and I got to the 1990s, Carol and I both remembered how horrible that decade was for her. She had tried, again and again, to reach me in those years, but I was numb and not reachable.

Lou had asked me, "What do you want from her?" But the opening Carol and I had experienced when I was married to Lou faded quickly into the background when I married Sam.

But, like me, Carol is relentless. We adhered to the process of storytelling—sticking with what happened in the world with other people, rather than the thoughts and emotions swirling in our own minds. Carol told me what she remembered, and I told her what I remembered. When we let the past be past, without judgements, we opened a new space where we were able to defuse the landmines of those years and sit peacefully again in the present.

Carol forced me to see moments I didn't want to see, stories from her own life that I will let her tell in her own way. For the first time we saw moments when we had caused one another pain, and remembering them did not create more pain. It was a miracle, really, how we dissolved the pain that had blocked our path for so long. And I often tell people now, "Carol and I have had more quality mother-daughter time this past year than in all of our years together." It was a gift we gave to one another through shared storytelling.

I came to see how I often ignored experiences that were too painful to talk about. And, in those times, my silence did even more damage than the original, painful events.

All of these feelings of inadequacy swirled around in my mind and came out in my dramatic attempts at healing and even more dramatic—and damaging—rituals of self-doubt and self-punishment. It was not easy to be my daughter during those years, and to live with the sense of having to fight for my attention and love.

Really, I think I was a better businesswoman and community leader than mother. Each of my daughters accepts this in me, but it took me a long time to accept it in myself. My fear of Carol, my inability to speak with her directly when she needed it most, damaged not only my relationship with Carol, but also Carol's relationship with Nan. It is as if that relationship stalled when their father died, and they are still both teenage girls, crying out for my love and yearning for his.

To Carol's credit, she never stopped trying to reach me, even in the dark years of my marriage to Sam. I just couldn't meet her as who she really was. And I was furious with her when she forgave him, after I decided to divorce him, and asked me to forgive him and move on as well. I wanted her to take my side, but she refused.

"I'm not forgiving what he did," she said at the time, "but I am forgiving him. It's not about him. I need to do that for my own healing. I will always be on your side, but I don't need to make him the enemy to do that."

I totally missed the power of what she was saying when she said it the first time.

But when she showed up and started listening to my story, with that same intention and without judgments, almost immediately things started to soften between us. And as we worked back through the decades that had passed without us really knowing one another or sharing one another's lives, we came to see and appreciate one another's perspectives. She saw how frail and frightened I was when her father was dying. I saw what I could not see then: that she and Nan were also in tremendous pain and had lost someone who believed in them unconditionally and unequivocally. In his last delirious days, they stuck by his side, trying to keep him alive. Carol was the last person to talk to Sy before he died.

Sy had separate, very memorable conversations with both girls the day before he died. He kept trying to get my attention, but I was too busy working, and preparing myself for the moment when I would need to move on, to hear the last message he wanted to leave with me.

***

So here we are, on the fifth day of Hanukkah 5778, the Jewish festival of miracles, each candle a reminder of how the divine spirit shows up in mysterious ways, extending a sliver of hope over time and space, creating the light and possibility of love. Go out, dear reader, and make your own miracles. This is my last and most important lesson:

Lesson #48: Bring hope and courage to others in these troubled times. That's why we're here; that's all we have; and it is enough.